INSIGHT POCKET GUIDE

Rome

W9-CFM-832

Discovery CHANNEL

APA PUBLICATIONS L
Part of the Langenscheidt Publishing Group

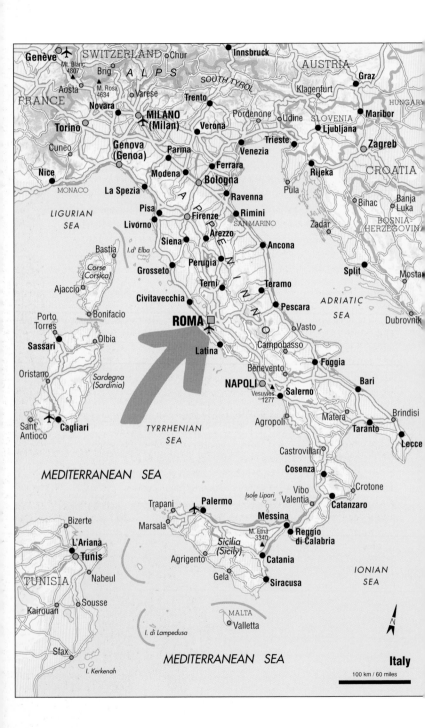

Italy

100 km / 60 miles

introduction

Welcome

This guidebook combines the interests and enthusiasms of two of the world's best-known information providers: Insight Guides, who have set the standard for visual travel guides since 1970, and Discovery Channel, the world's premier source of non-fiction television programming. To this end, it brings you the best of Rome in a series of tailor-made itineraries.

Ancient Romans' Rome, now visible only at the Forum, lies 4 metres (13ft) under the new one. But that's only one of the two great empires this city has nurtured. The Rome of the Church has the Vatican and its fabulous museums, as well as more than 2,000 churches – Romanesque, Renaissance, baroque – and probably just as many palaces, built by people of secular as well as ecclesiastical power and fame.

In these pages, one of Insight's regular writers and editors, John Wilcock, and Rome correspondent Angelo Quattrocchi peel back the city's many layers to help visitors get the most out of their stay. The guide comprises 11 city tours, the first four focusing on the key areas of Centro Storico, the archaeological zone, the Vatican and Trastevere, and the next seven, shorter itineraries exploring other interesting areas and aspects of the city. These are followed by an *Excursions* section suggesting four worthwhile trips to towns and sights within easy reach of Rome.

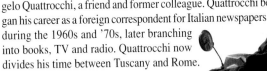

John Wilcock, an internationally-known journalist who blazed a career from his native Yorkshire through such publications as *The New York Times* and *Village Voice*, has travelled the world for Insight. He was delighted that *Insight Pocket Guide: Rome* should give him the chance to team up with Angelo Quattrocchi, a friend and former colleague. Quattrocchi began his career as a foreign correspondent for Italian newspapers during the 1960s and '70s, later branching into books, TV and radio. Quattrocchi now divides his time between Tuscany and Rome.

Preceding Pages: Ponte Sant'Angelo
Following Pages: fanfare in Piazza Quirinale

History & Culture

history/culture

Nearly everybody is familiar with the legend of the founding of ancient Rome: the twin sons of the war god Mars were abandoned then saved by a she-wolf who suckled them. The babies were later found and nurtured by a poor shepherd and his wife. When they grew up, the twins traced the outlines of the city with a sacred plough and then quarrelled over it. Romulus killed his brother, Remus, and named the city after himself. There is even a precise date attributed to its founding – 21 April, 753BC. Far-fetched as this might sound, the date has gained some credence: archaeologists excavating the Palatine hill claim that the 'huts of Romulus' date from about that era and probably belonged to Etruscan, Sabine and Latin settlers.

The 1st-century writer Livy, who produced 140 books under the rubric *History of Rome*, endorses the tale of Romulus who, he wrote, invited all the neighbouring tribes to a big festival so that all the women could be kidnapped. This 'Rape of the Sabine Women' was 'a marvellous story', in the opinion of Livy and a worthy complement to his thesis that 'if any nation deserves the privilege of claiming divine ancestry, that nation is our own.' Gradually the city spread over the six surrounding hills: the Capitoline, Viminal, Esquiline, Caelian, Aventine and Quirinal.

A Ruling Triumvirate

Tarquinius, the first Etruscan king, was succeeded by several others before the Etruscans were sent packing with the military defeat of their seventh king, Tarquinius Superbus, in the early years of the 6th century BC. A republic was proclaimed in 509BC, and it was decided that two consuls, elected annually, should run the community. This became a triumvirate (Pompey, Crassus and Julius Caesar) in 65BC following seven years of Pompey's rule. Next it was Caesar who assumed authority, but only for a year or two before he was murdered by jealous colleagues.

Caesar's dalliance with the young Egyptian queen, Cleopatra, his political dominance and his inevitable assassination form one of the most dramatic and oft-told tales in world history. Shakespeare's version is probably the most famous. Here he portrays Cassius persuading Brutus to join the plot against Caesar:

'Why, man, he doth bestride the narrow world
Like a Colossus, and we petty men
Walk under his huge legs, and peep about
To find ourselves dishonourable graves.
Men at some time are masters of their fates:
The fault, dear Brutus, is not in our stars,
But in ourselves, that we are underlings.
Brutus and Caesar: what should be in that "Caesar"?
Why should that name be sounded more than yours?'

Left: daily life in the Forum as depicted by a 19th-century artist
Right: a powerful figure

After the defeat and deaths of the conspirators, and through the decade that followed, a second triumvirate comprising Caesar's nephew Octavian, Mark Antony and Lepidus (who had served as one of Caesar's generals) maintained control. But during that time and for a decade afterwards the republic was racked with dissent, to the point of civil war. Following her fling with Caesar,  Cleopatra had a romance with Mark Antony, as well; the Egyptian ruler had tasted power and liked it. But after Augustus – as Octavian now called himself – expropriated her fortune and defeated Antony at Actium, she killed herself. Augustus's 41-year reign was a golden age. He established an efficient civil service, Rome's brilliant engineers built an infrastructure that was to last for hundreds of years (some of it still exists) and writers such as Ovid, Virgil and Livy were at work. After Augustus's death, he was deified by the senate, and shrines were set up throughout the empire.

Bread and Circuses

There followed a succession of tyrannical emperors – Tiberius, Caligula, Claudius and Nero – before Vespasian (AD69–79) seized the reins and restored order to the tangled state. In addition to inventing the pay toilet (a novel way to collect taxes), he also built the Colosseum, the biggest entertainment complex of its time. 'Bread and circuses' was the judgement of Juvenal, the 1st-century poet, on the way the city's rulers kept the populace happy. The 18th-century historian Edward Gibbon described the period after Mark Antony's death as 'a revolution which will ever be remembered and is still felt by the nations of the earth'. Gibbon's multi-volume *The History of the Decline and Fall of the Roman Empire* explains how the structure of this society gradually fell apart. The emperor Diocletian split Rome's imperial legacy into two parts, and Constantine subsequently decided to move the capital east to Byzantium, later called Constantinople.

Though Diocletian (AD284–305) was tolerant towards Christianity, the emperor Julian (361–3) made a short-lived attempt to restore paganism. His successor, Theodosius, made Christianity Rome's official religion in 380. This edict was not revoked until late in the 20th century. Meanwhile the Christian Church was becoming ambitious. Sensing a power vacuum created by the emperor's absence from Rome, it sought temporal as well as spiritual authority, but its grab for control was premature.

Over the centuries, different waves of barbarians invaded and sacked the city. Successive popes embarked upon strategic alliances in their efforts to repulse the invaders, but they were rarely successful. The last would-be Caesar was the Goth invader Totila who, after taking over the city in AD546, staged the final chariot races in the Circus Maximus three years later. Pope Formosus (891–6) and the five popes who succeeded him reduced the papacy to its lowest ebb. In medieval times Rome was subject to internal strife. In 1200 it became an independent commune under Arnaldo di Breschia, who tried unsuccessfully to bring back a Roman republic complete with consuls and a senate. He paid a terrible price for his republicanism: he was overthrown, tortured and hanged.

In 1300 Pope Boniface ordained the Church's first jubilee, which enticed so many pilgrims to Rome that it became, from 1350, a regular event, celebrated every 25 years. With the consecration of Pope Clement V at Lyon in 1305, the papacy was in effect hijacked by the French; it was transported to Avignon, where it remained for the next 70 years. Pilgrims had long been Rome's major source of revenue. As far back as the 6th century, Pope Gregory I, inventor of the Gregorian chant, had contemplated the idea of destroying Rome's antiquities 'to concentrate the minds of visitors on spiritual matters'. Despite Petrarch's assessment that Rome was 'a shapeless heap of ruins', pilgrims began flooding in at the rate of 5,000 a day.

The Renaissance

In the 15th and 16th centuries, the glory of imperial Rome was born again as an inspiration for those wealthy patrons who could tell the artists in their charge exactly what they wanted to see on their canvases. Classical Rome became the mainspring of the Renaissance, many of whose artists and writers 'laboured to restore the vast ruins and broken buildings of antiquity [as well as] the texts of its literature', as James Bruce Ross and Mary Martin McLaughlin put it in *The Portable Renaissance Reader* (Penguin, 1968).

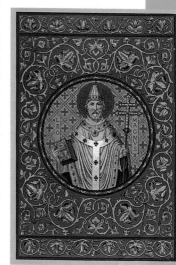

Many of the glorious palaces of Rome and Florence date from this era and, following the lead of their predecessors, Nicholas V (who began work on the Basilica of St Peter's) and Sixtus IV (who commissioned the Sistine Chapel), as well as Julius II (1503–13), supported the work of artists such as Raphael and Michelangelo. Suddenly, painters who had previously

Above left: history's most famous she-wolf
Left: Emperor Augustus. **Right**: Pope Leo I

ranked alongside humble artisans were catapulted into a far more prestigious status, and found themselves mingling with the aristocracy.

In the 16th century, Vatican favourites Gianlorenzo Bernini and his rival Francesco Borromini filled the city with sumptuous churches and palaces, stat-

ues and fountains to glorify the Holy See. They left a timeless legacy of magnificent art which, it must be said, helped to emphasise the disparity between the immense wealth and extravagance of the Church and the poverty of its parishioners. And yet, for all the Church's riches, Italy itself was even more prosperous – it had long been the envy of other European powers.

With the traitorous assistance of Milan's rulers and the support of the fanatical Dominican friar Savonarola in Florence, the French King Charles V invaded Italy in 1495 and battled with Italian troops at the village of Fornovo. 'If the Italians had won at Fornovo,' wrote Luigi Barzini in *The Italians*, 'they would probably have discovered then the pride of being a united people.' But the dream of Italian unification was still three centuries away. The defeat left Italy and its magnificent prizes vulnerable to the predatory intentions of half the nations of Europe.

Spain emerged as the new power in Italy, and the papacy was, once again, only too happy to endorse its victory: Pope Clement VII crowned Spain's Charles V as Holy Roman Emperor in 1530. Charles and his descendants ruled Italy with a heavy hand for the next century and a half.

Napoleon's Army

Then it was Napoleon's turn. 'The French army comes to break your chains,' he declared. '...we make war as generous enemies and we have no quarrel save with tyrants who enslave you.' Having defeated the papal forces at Ancona, Napoleon demanded money and artworks from the Vatican, took Pope Pius VI across the border into France and married off his sister, Maria Pauline, to Prince Camillo Borghese. The prince responded by selling the Borghese family's art treasures for 30 million francs, a bargain job-lot that formed the basis of the Louvre's collection. In 1808, after Pope Pius VII stubbornly refused to cooperate with Napoleon, French troops returned to occupy Rome. The pope was sent into exile in Savona and later in Fontainebleu. He was not to return for another six years.

The long struggle of the Risorgimento – the rise of Italian nationalism and the unification of the Italian states – began in 1820. Such patriots as

Above: Carpaccio's *Meeting with the Pope*
Right: Rome in the 18th century

Giuseppe Garibaldi (1807–82) and Giuseppe Mazzini (1805–72) were dedicated to uniting the disparate states. Mazzini, founder of a movement called La Giovana Italia, proclaimed a Roman republic in 1849, but the French were not going to give up up quite that easily. Supported by Pope Pius IX, France invaded Rome once again. Supporters of unification had proclaimed the birth of a kingdom of Italy, with Sardinia's ruler, Victor Emmanuel III, as king, and with the pope and the papal state confined to a suburb, in the 1860s. In 1870 the French left and the king's troops finally entered the city.

Benito Mussolini

In May 1871, parliament tried to make peace with the papacy by passing the Law of Guarantees, which allowed the Church to retain the Vatican city. But Pope Pius IX was having none of it. He refused to accept the law and, excommunicated its authors. When Italy entered World War I, on the side of the Allies, in 1915, the stand-off between Church and state showed no signs of reaching a resolution. The friction continued until 1929, when Mussolini's Fascist regime signed the Lateran Treaty with the Vatican, represented by Cardinal Gaspari. The Church was compensated for the loss of its rights, and given authority over about 44 ha (110 acres) of Vatican property, including the papal villa at Castel Gandolfo.

World War I left Benito Mussolini, the former editor of a Socialist newspaper, 'burning with patriotism and bursting with ambition… shrinking from no violence or brutality, a born master of conspiracy'. He named his party the Fascisti after the *fasces*, the rods that symbolised a magistrate's authority in ancient Rome. In 1922 he marched on the capital, ostensibly to save the country from Bolshevism. His black-shirted stormtroopers silenced critics by forcing castor oil down their throats. With the king allowed a nominal position on the throne, Mussolini bulldozed a number of measures into law. Rome's streets were widened to 'make room for the dignity, the hygiene and the beauty of the capital. It is necessary', he said, 'to reconcile the demands of ancient and modern Rome.'

World War II and its Aftermath

Mussolini took Italy into World War II on 9 June, 1940, when he felt confident that Germany would be victorious. Hitler, at first ambivalent about Mussolini's value as an ally, came to think of him as a liability. 'It is in fact quite obvious,' he grumbled, 'that our Italian alliance has been of more service to our enemies than to ourselves.' Eventually the Nazi leader found it necessary to despatch the German army to occupy Rome. The German forces were, to some extent, frustrated by the Italian resistance, to which they replied with ruthless reprisals. Thousands died, including 335 killed in a mass murder at the Regina Coeli prison, before the Germans withdrew. Mussolini was hanged by partisans in the north, where Hitler had installed him as a puppet governor.

For four decades after the war Rome was a mess, physically and spiritually. The most notable feature of its shaky infrastructure was unrestricted jerry-building, and there was widespread political, commercial and criminal corruption. The papacy was not exempt from scandal and sudden death. (Pope John Paul I enjoyed only a month in office before he died.)

In 1992, the start of an anti-corruption campaign known as *Mani Pulite* ('Clean Hands') resulted in the jailing of 1,000 businessmen and accusations against hundreds of politicians and industrialists. Despite an outbreak of terrorism the following year, instigated by the Mafia and supporters of the status quo, there were signs of a moral resurgence in public life. In 1995 the new *Mani Pulite* party pledged to restore the moral fabric.

In the closing years of the 1990s, the city concentrated on the celebrations for the Rome 2000 jubilee – marking the start of Christianity's third millennium. The influx of millions of pilgrims in this landmark year put great pressure on Rome's city planners. In the five-year period leading up to the millennium jubilee (inaugurated by the Pope's ceremonial opening of the Holy Door at St Peter's Basilica), Rome's superstructure was considerably enhanced. For example, new metro stations have extended the A line beyond the Vatican stop at Ottaviano, thereby improving the local transport system and easing congestion caused by the sheer number of visitors. At the same time there have been demands to improve living conditions of the three-quarters of Rome's 2.8 million citizens who reside in those grim suburbs which bear little resemblance to the breathtakingly lovely centre.

Above: Mussolini salutes his supporters
Right: a Roman citizen

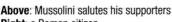

HISTORY HIGHLIGHTS

753BC According to legend, Romulus founds Rome and becomes its first king.

509BC Fall of the seventh Etruscan king, Tarquinius Superbus. End of Etruscan rule. Republic proclaimed.

387BC Gauls conquer Rome.

312–308BC Appius Claudius builds the Appian Way.

241BC Victory in the First Punic War. Sicily becomes a Roman province.

218BC Second Punic War. Hannibal crosses the Alps.

216BC Defeat at Cannae. Hannibal *ante portas* (before the gates).

202BC Decisive victory over Hannibal in Battle of Zama ends war.

146BC Destruction of Carthage and Corinth.

133BC Civil war starts with the murder of Tiberius Gracchus.

101BC First clash with the Germans; Cimberi and Teutons wiped out.

71BC Gladiatorial War led by Spartacus ends in bloodbath.

60BC First triumvirate: Caesar, Pompey, Crassus.

51BC Caesar accomplishes his conquest of Gaul.

44BC Caesar assassinated.

43BC Second triumvirate: Antony, Octavian, Aemilius Lepidus.

31BC Caesar Octavian Augustus assumes autocracy.

9BC Danube border established.

AD64 First persecution of Christians under Emperor Nero.

98 Trajan takes up office. The empire is extended.

270 Aurelian builds a defensive wall round Rome.

286 Diocletian divides empire's administration into east and west.

330 Constantinople becomes capital of the empire.

410 Alarich, leader of the West Goths, plunders Rome.

452 Pope Leo the Great prevents Attila from conquering Rome.

546 Totila, king of the East Goths, conquers Rome.

800 Coronation of Charlemagne as Roman Emperor.

1144 Arnaldo di Breschia tries – like Cola di Rienzo later – to separate Rome from the papacy.

1300 Boniface VIII organises the first 'Holy Year'. Papacy at the height of its power.

1309 Clement V chooses Avignon as his residence. Papacy falls under the influence of French kings.

1378 The 'Avignon exile' ends with the election of Urban VI of Rome. Clement VII sets up as counter-pope.

1417 The election of Martin V ends 40 years of schism; the pope is once again ruler of Rome.

1527 *Sacco di Roma*: German and Spanish mercenaries plunder the city for months, 30,000 die.

1572 Gregory XIII begins restoration of ancient water pipes; the Roman fountain tradition begins.

1797 General Duphot raises the 'Roman Republic'.

1815 The Roman Church state is restored by Congress of Vienna.

1860 A large part of the Church state falls to the kingdom of Italy.

1870 Rome, population 20,000, is conquered by Spanish troops and becomes capital of Italy.

1922 Fascists march on Rome. Mussolini becomes dictator.

1944 Allied troops march into the city on 4 July.

1957 The Treaty of Rome is signed on 25 March, laying the foundation for a united Europe.

1994 Thirty-year rule by the alliance between the Christian Democrats and the Socialists is defeated by the 'Clean Hands' movement.

2000 Rome 2000 jubilee celebrates the start of Christianity's third millennium.

Central Rome

500 m / 550 yds

Itinerary 1
Itinerary 2
Itinerary 5
Itinerary 6
Itinerary 9

City Itineraries

The city of Rome, which is thousands of years old, is really two cities: the centre and the suburbs. The centre comprises palaces, churches, piazzas and tree-lined avenues, or *viali*, on what is left of the original seven hills (one of which is now topped by a Hilton hotel). Big *portas* (arches) open into the famous Roman roads: the Aurelia, north to the sea; the Cassia, north to Viterbo and Florence; the Flaminia, north to Umbria; the Salaria, northeast to Abruzzi. The Tiburtina runs south to Tivoli and the hills called Castelli; the Tuscolana and the Appia Antica, south to Naples. The Tiber, bisecting the city, runs 24km (15 miles) west to the port of Ostia.

The itineraries section of this guide begins with four tours focusing on the main sights of ancient Rome, medieval Rome, Renaissance Rome and the Vatican, and aims to capture the city's essential flavour. The remaining city-based tours cover other interesting areas of the city, while a separate Excursions section suggests visits to towns and villages near the city. Don't try to cram everything into a couple of days; to do the city justice, you should aim to spend around a week here.

1. ART HISTORIANS' ROME *(see map, p18–19)*

Start in Piazza Navona, visit a number of lovely churches and, from Roman times, the Pantheon, admire Bernini sculptures and a painting by Caravaggio, see the Trevi Fountain, the Spanish Steps and the Villa Borghese, and end the tour in the Piazza del Popolo.

What is now the **Piazza Navona** was built in the 1st century by the Emperor Domitian as a track for chariot racing (a sport in which losers ran the risk of execution). It retains its original shape, enhanced by the baroque buildings that surround it. The piazza's centrepiece is the magnificent **Fountain of the Rivers**, whose fine sculptures by papal favourite Gianlorenzo Bernini (1598–1680) represent the Danube, Rio de la Plata, Ganges and the Nile. The Nile's head is symbolically veiled, and its upraised hand points to the church of **Sant' Agnese**, built seven years later by Bernini's rival, Francesco Borromini. When, in 1651, the fountain was unveiled, not a drop of water was to be seen and a dejected Pope Innocent X (whose coat of arms it bears) began to walk away. Only then did Bernini dramatically turn on the tap. The pope turned back, delighted.

Pigeons, souvenir salesmen ('your name on a grain of rice'), artists and tourists alike are irresistably drawn to the fountain, and the piazza's extravagantly expensive restaurants are usually very crowded.

Left: St Peter and the key to heaven
Right: Fontana del Nettuno

Opposite the fountain at the piazza's southern end is a Bernini sea god. Exit here, via di Lorenesi, cross Anima and enter **Santa Maria dell' Anima,** the German national church at the rear. After ringing the bell, you will find, in the dimly-lit interior, a treasure trove of glorious frescoes. The one behind

the altar is by Giuliano Romano, a pupil of Raphael. A famous painting by the master himself, *Four Sybils*, sits in the adjoining **Santa Maria della Pace** but this has long been closed for restoration. This warren of backstreets is full of innumerable antiques stores and cafés, the best-known of which, the ivy-covered **Caffé della Pace**, has no outside sign to mark its presence. Next door, in Via del Fico, the **Caffé del Fico** is the trendiest of the local intellectual hangouts.

The Pasquino Statue

Adjoining Sant' Agnese church on the piazza is the **Palazzo Pamphili** (Pamphili Palace), which is now the Brazilian embassy. This building owes its origin to Pope Innocent X, a member of the Pamphili family, whose name also adorns the gorgeous villa and gardens behind the Gianicolo. The palace contains a gallery built by Borromini. A famous resident of the palace was the pope's sister-in-law, Olympia, whose unpopularity around the Rome of her day was reflected in graffiti scrawled on the **Pasquino statue** on the corner opposite the building. Pasquino, a local shoemaker and no respecter of the Church, established the custom of attaching anti-papal messages to the old Hellenistic marble statue and the practice continued through the centuries.

Leaving Navona from the side opposite the church, you are confronted by the 400-year-old **Madama Palace,** built for the Medici family, two of whose members became popes. It was named for Margarethe of Austria, the bastard daughter of Charles V, who married first Alessandro de' Medici and then, on his death, Ottavio Farnese. As a consequence of this liaison, the fabulous Medici art collection was split between the two dynastic families. One block right along the Corso del Rinascimento, at the Archivo di Stato sign, pass through the courtyard, pausing at Borromino's twisted spire on the church of **Sant' Ivo** (usually closed), leaving via the dark alley on the right. Two blocks left along Via Dogana Vecchia is the church of **San Luigi dei Francesi**, with works by Caravaggio in the fifth chapel on the right. Brawler, gambler and convicted killer, Caravaggio (1573–1610) is admired for his use of chiaroscuro and his realistic depiction of religious subjects.

Across the street a sign points along Via Giustiniani to the **Pantheon**

Above: the Pantheon
Right: the Spanish Steps

(open mornings only), the best-preserved of all the Roman temples, despite being gutted by several popes. Most notoriously, Urban VIII melted down its bronze girders to make cannons. The structure, built during the reign of Hadrian (AD118–125) in place of an earlier temple built by Agrippa, is still very impressive. Its 43.3-m (140-ft) wide dome is so high that the circle of light at the summit seems scarcely bigger than a rabbit hole. After Raphael's death in 1520 his request to be buried in this building was granted.

The street along the Pantheon's south side passes the statue of an elephant topped with an obelisk, designed by Bernini, to **Santa Maria Sopra Minerva**. Here there are lots of famous tombs, including those of two Medici popes and the Dominican monk Fra Angelico, whose 15th-century art is renowned for its bright colours and matchless piety. Near the altar are frescoes by the Renaissance artist Filippino Lippi, and a statue by Michelangelo.

Column of Marcus Aurelius

Return to the Pantheon, a short way beyond which is the cheap and cheerful pizzeria **La Maddalena**. After lunch, continue along Via Maddalena, turning right along Uffici del Vicario. At this point you might want to stop at the renowned ice-cream parlour **Giolitti** before turning into Piazza di Montecitorio. Here and in the adjoining Piazza Colonna stand the buildings of the Italian parliament and senate. The startling **Column of Marcus Aurelius** is engraved with reliefs depicting the successes of this 2nd-century emperor's military campaigns. Though the column was restored in 1988, the spiral staircase in its interior is no longer used. After crossing the Corso en route to the Fontana di Trevi, turn one block to the right to see the venerable **Sciarra Gallery** with its bizarre mix of architectural styles.

The **Trevi Fountain**, one of Rome's most popular sights, was built in 1736 and funnels water from an aqueduct that is more than 2,000 years old.

The fountain found new fame as a result of Fellini's groundbreaking 1960 movie *La Dolce Vita*, in which Anita Ekberg used it for a midnight bathe. But of course it's most famous for the legend: throw a coin into the water and you ensure that one day you will return to the eternal city.

Not long ago, the owners of the building housing the Hotel Fontana were offering to sell just the ground floor for a mere £8 million. Another well-known landmark, the **Piazza di Spagna**, is about 20 minutes' walk from here, along Lavatore to Due Macelli. Most famous of all, the Spanish Steps are crowded throughout the year, but in summer their appeal is augmented by a pretty, fragrant bonus: they are lined with flowers. Residents and visitors alike come here to patronise American Express or McDonald's. The popularity of these American institutions isn't that surprising when you consider that the quaint English tearoom, **Babington's**, charges L28,000 (£13/$20) for Welsh rarebit, and 8,600 (£4/$6) for a bottle of Coca-Cola.

Villa Medici

Three parallel streets that spin off from the piazza – Frattina, Condotti and Borgognona – attract Rome's most upmarket shoppers with such famous brand names as Armani, Gucci, Bulgari and Cartier. At the top of the Spanish Steps and to the left is the **Villa Medici**, built at the top of the former Gardens of Lucullus. These days the villa houses the French Academy, whose students have included the composers Berlioz and Debussy, and the artist Fragonard. The fountain was famously sketched by the German polymath Goethe

in 1787. At the very top of the incline, in the park of the **Villa Borghese**, is one of the most popular eating places among visiting dignitaries, the **Casina Valadier**, which is surrounded by busts of statesmen, artists and writers.

It was the architect Giuseppe Valadier who laid out the impressive **Piazza del Popolo** below. In the centre is an Egyptian obelisk which Augustus originally had installed in the Circus Maximus. The Via del Corso ends here in 25-m (82-ft) high red-brick walls that mark the boundary of the ancient city. The Corso runs across Rome in a straight line to Mussolini's hideous Monument to Victor Emmanuel, which Romans deride as *La Macchina da Scrivete* ('the typewriter'). At the station across from the Piazza del Popolo you can take a train north to medieval Viterbo (2½ hours), which was the home of the pope in the 13th century. Alternatively, the train will take you to such delightful villages as Sacrofano or Soriano del Cimino.

The least expensive official 'tour' in Rome is a trip across the city on the 116 electric bus from near the Principe Amedeo bridge.

Above: a Greek temple in the Villa Borghese

2. ANCIENT ROME *(see map, p18–19)*

The city's origins by the Palatine hill; Michelangelo's piazza and the Capitoline museums; the Forum, Colosseum and Circus Maximus.

Surrounded as it is by buildings and statues by Michelangelo, there's no better place to start exploring ancient Rome than the **Campidoglio** – then, as now, the seat of the city's government. Here stood the immense bronze statue of Marcus Aurelius, today placed in the courtyard to your left behind glass panels designed to protect it from pollution. The corridors of the **Palazzo del Museo Capitolino** are lined with statues and busts of mythical figures such as Bacchus, Cupid and Psyche, and of prominent Romans of the day. A justly famous piece is the *Red Faun*, a rosy marble version of the Greek original that belonged to Hadrian, who built the villa at Tivoli and who, of all Rome's emperors, was most sympathetic to the ancient Greek civilisation. At a mere 50m (64ft) in height, the Capitoline is the lowest of Rome's seven hills; the Campidoglio (Italian for 'Capitol') that stands on it was once a sanctuary for the persecuted called the Asylum.

The **Palazzo dei Conservatori** on the right deserves more of your time. Its many masterpieces include the Etruscan she-wolf suckling Romulus and Remus, and a 1st-century sculpture of a boy taking a thorn out of his foot. Stretching right up to the 12-m (40-ft) high ceiling of one room, a mural records the days when battling tribes would settle disputes by delegating gladiators to represent them. On the occasion represented by the mural, two Romans were killed, but the third ran fast enough to outpace his enemies, turning to kill them one by one.

Upstairs, in the first room, see the wonderful *Portrait of a Young Woman* by Domenico Paneoti (*circa* 1480) and, in the adjoining room, *Portrait of a*

Above: Piazza del Campidoglio
Left: Marcus Aurelius in bronze

Man by Giovanni Bellini, the dominant Venetian painter of the 15th century. Tintoretto and Bassano are also represented in this room, as is Paolo Calliani (1528–88) with his *Rape of Europa*. Reni's self-portrait is next to the very large painting of Romulus and Remus by Peter Paul Rubens (1577–1640).

Turn right as you leave the museums and walk down Via del Campidoglio, past the town hall, for an overview of the **Forum.** Over to the left is the **Arch of Septimius Severus**, which in AD203 was the venue for celebrations marking the first decade of the reluctant emperor's reign. Nearby, eight pillars remain of the **Temple of Saturn**, which housed the state treasury, and three pillars of the **Temple of Vespasian** (who built the Colosseum). It was the custom of generals and emperors to erect columns and arches to celebrate their victories and, beginning with Caesar, some built entirely new forums.

Remembering Caesar

There was a tendency for the populace to regard emperors as gods when they died and this was certainly the case with Caesar, in whose memory Augustus erected a temple. It still stands, on the spot where Caesar was cremated after his assassination in 44BC. Augustus became a godlike figure during his 41-year reign, assuming the title of Pontifex Maximus that was afterwards adopted by the popes. Cleopatra's wealth was expropriated by Augustus who used it to transform Rome from 'a city of brick into a city of marble' – whose remains you see in the Forum. Not even centuries of neglect, or the subsequent denudation by Renaissance architects, who dismantled buildings to incorporate the materials into their palaces, has lessened its majesty.

Close to Caesar's temple is one devoted to **Vesta**, goddess of the hearth and patron of the state. Chosen from good families with impeccable pedigrees, the ladies who became Vestal Virgins watched over a sacred image of Minerva (daughter of Jupiter and Juno) and kept the flame alight through

Above: the remains of the massive statue of Constantine

wind and storm. They each served a term of 30 years and were obliged to remain inviolate on pain of death (their lovers were strangled). In return for their faithful service they were honoured everywhere, travelling in wheeled carriages and favoured with the best seats on all public occasions.

Tarpeian Rock

Next to the **Temple of Castor and Pollux**, the twin sons of Jupiter, is the **Temple of Caesar**. Other notable edifices here include the **Basilica of Constantine**, about halfway up the left-hand side, where a colossal statue was found in 1487. Long since broken up, its hands and feet stand in the courtyard of the museum. At the far end, near the rebuilt **Arch of Titus**, are the extensive ruins of the **Temple of Venus and Rome** designed by the Emperor Hadrian in AD125, destroyed by fire in 307 and rebuilt by Maxentius. Up the hill to the right from where you stand is the **Tarpeian Rock**, named for the 8th-century BC traitor Tarpeia who let the besieging Sabines, led by her lover King Titus Tatius, into Rome. (They were swiftly ejected and Tarpeia herself was crushed to death between the soldiers' shields). The rock became a landmark from which traitors would be tossed.

Head back out of the piazza and down the stairway. Viewed from across the street, the two sets of adjacent stairways are an impressive sight, but the 125 wide marble steps leading up to the Aracoeli church are steeper and higher. They were built in the 14th century, when the church was already 100 years old, and according to legend they bring good fortune to the buyer of a lottery ticket who is willing to climb them on his knees. **Santa Maria in Aracoeli**, at the top, sits on the site of a temple dedicated to Juno where Augustus later built an altar. Juno's full name was Jupiter Moneda, whence comes our word 'money' – her temple was the site of the earliest mint. Geese were sacred to Juno; their honking is said to have warned the Romans of an attack by the Gauls in 390BC. The church contains Pinturicchio paintings of scenes from the life of Siena's St Bernardino.

The **Via dei Fori Imperiali** leading beyond the Colosseum to the Appian Way, the major route to the south, was built by Mussolini, who had acres of ruins cleared for the project. In a rush to show the results of his ambitious plans, Il Duce lacked the patience to investigate a potential treasure-trove of antiquity. Thousands of people were evicted, and with them went the remains of innumerable temples, arches and palaces.

At the opposite side of the broad street are forums built by Augustus, Caesar and Nerva, the emperor who in AD96 succeeded Domitian but whose rule lasted for a mere two years. Here also are the astonishing markets of Nerva's successor, Trajan, who in AD106 hired the best architect of his time, Apollodorus of Damascus, to create what was in effect a 2nd-century mall offering one-stop shopping.

At the eastern end of **Trajan's Market** is a huge Renaissance palace that, though built 1,300 years later, blends perfectly because, of course, the Renaissance was inspired by classical Rome, whose aesthetic it strove to reproduce.

Right: a Vestal Virgin

The Colosseum

Living on the plunder of the empire and spending money freely, the imperial rulers kept the masses distracted on a diet of 'bread and circuses'. In the **Colosseum** 55,000 spectators could be entertained at once. The Colosseum (open daily) stands on the site of what was Nero's artificial lake, 188m (617ft) long by 156m (512ft) wide and opened in AD80 with three months of games. Christians fought lions, gladiators fought each other and wounded contestants lived or died according to the emperor's whim, expressed by the imperial thumb, which pointed either up or down. Gladiators were usually prisoners or slaves who, along with the animals, waited their turn in the warren of rooms and corridors beneath the arena.

As founder of the Colosseum, Vespasian (AD69–79) was the PT Barnum of his time. Having succeeded Nero (who died as a result of his excesses), he took the site from his predecessor's estate. As late as the 16th century, relics of the Nero era were still turning up on his former property. The Laocoon statue (now in the Vatican museum) was discovered here – 1,200 years after Pliny the Elder first catalogued it.

Homes for Top Romans

The **Palatine**, which can also be reached via the Arch of Titus in the Forum, was the roosting place of numerous top Romans: Catullus and Cicero, as well as the emperors Augustus, Tiberius, Caligula, Nero, Domitian and Septimius Severus built homes here, near a temple to the moon goddess Cybele. 'We honour men by speaking, the gods by silence,' wrote Plutarch, possibly referring to the no-talking rule observed in Cybele's temple.

Just east of the headless statue of Cybele, behind the **Temple of Apollo** remains was the house of Augustus and his wife Livia with frescoes dated to around that emperor's time. According to the biographer Suetonius, Augustus lived simply in this modest house for 40 years. Of the rooms gradually added, most were used for public functions. Nero's extravagant **Domus Aurea** (Golden House), built in AD64 and described by Seutonius and Tacitus in glowing terms, recently opened to the public for the first time in 2000 years (summer 9am–8pm; winter hours to be decided; tel: 06-4815576 for information; tel: 06-39749907 for reservations). With its lake, vegetable garden and menagerie, it once covered most of the area between the Palatine and Oppian hills and was splendidly decorated with gold, silver and precious stones. Close to the entrance of the palace stood an enormous bronze statue of Nero standing 37 metres (121 ft) high.

The biggest palace on the Palatine was that of Domitian (whose Arch of Titus in the Forum honoured both his brother and his father Vespasian).

Above: the Temple of Caesar
Right: the Colosseum

The public wing, **Domus Flavia**, was the main imperial palace for the next three centuries. Its surviving walls are still impressive. Domitian's living quarters were in the other wing, the **Domus Augustana** where, despite his justifiably paranoid precautions, he was killed in AD96. The huge **stadium** dates from the same period.

The other major attraction on the Palatine hill is the **botanical garden**, which Pope Paul III's grandson, Cardinal Farnese, built in the mid-1500s over the ruins of Tiberius's palace.

Circus Maximus

Between the Palatine and Aventine hills is the empty, open space of the **Circus Maximus**. Though said to have been built in the 7th century BC, its fame rests on the mock battles and chariot races of the era beginning with Julius Caesar. The long, grassy hollow, banked at one side, hasn't seen a chariot race since AD549 and today it's a pedestrian walkway between the Palatine and the circular **Temple of Hercules**. With its distinctive pillars, this is the oldest marble building in the city. Nearby is the 1st-century BC **Temple of Portunus,** god of rivers and ports. Collectively these temples close to the Tiber are known as the Forum Boarium, the name referring to the cattle market that stood here when the area was the site of Rome's first river port. Just across the street, **Bocca della Verità** ('the mouth of truth') is a stone head in the foyer of **Santa Maria in Cosmedin** church. Tourists enjoy putting their hands in the mouth – legend avers that the hand will be bitten off if they tell a lie.

If you head up along the river to finish this tour beside the **Fabricio** bridge, which crosses over to the island of Tiberina, you'll see to the right the massive **Theatre of Marcellus**. The theatre's massive curved wall features in a famous 19th-century print by Thomas Hartley Cromek, much reproduced on postcards. Marcellus was the nephew of the emperor Augustus, who dedicated the theatre to him after his premature death – he was still in his teens. The theatre was said to have been a model for the Colosseum, but much of the original building was incorporated into the 16th-century palace built by Baldassare Peruzzi for the Orsini family.

city itineraries

3. TRASTEVERE *(see map, p31)*

A casual stroll through the Bohemian Quarter, starting at the Sisto bridge, stopping at recommended restaurants and (on Sunday) the flea market. The day ends with a far-reaching view from the Gianicolo hill.

For many visitors Trastevere is the most colourful neighbourhood in the city. Meandering from the Tiber's Left Bank to the Gianicolo, it is Rome's equivalent of New York's Greenwich Village. In the wake of artists and writers has come an influx of jewellery and leather stores, cute bistros and nightclubs, but on the whole Trastevere ('across the Tiber') remains remarkably unspoiled. It is still the residential area it has been for a number of centuries. Mingling with the new residents of alternative lifestyles are born-and-bred locals who have never crossed the Tiber in their lives.

Beginning at the **Ponte Sisto**, descend the steps to admire the **Acqua**

Paola fountain, its inscription crediting Pope Pius VIII with providing water to bring his flock 'cleanliness and joy'. (Among Pius's other good works, incidentally, was the launch of the efficient Vatican postal service).

The flood-barrier walls were built in the 1930s by Mussolini. Unfortunately they prevent navigation, though every July a solitary tourist boat sails from Ponte Garibaldi – the next bridge down – all the way to the sea at Ostia. Until the embankments were built in the 19th century, there were still traces of the old port, the Ripa Romea, where Vatican-bound pilgrims arrived by boat.

The boat-shaped **Tiber Island**, reached by the Ponte Fabricio (built in 62BC) from one side and the Ponte Cestio (built 20 years later) from the other, is the river's sole island. It is mostly taken up by a hospital and has been associated with healing ever since, according to legend, Asclepius sent a boatload of magical snakes to the island to cure those suffering from the plague. By the river on the Trastevere side, the high embankment offers a delightful place to relax. Sit with your back to the wall when the sun is high in the sky and take in the Roman atmosphere.

Flea Market

Viale di Trastevere, the district's central thoroughfare, begins at the Garibaldi bridge. The medieval **Torre degli Anguillar** is to the left of the life-size statue of the 19th-century Roman satirist Giuseppe Belli. If it's a Sunday morning, continue along the Viale for about seven blocks, then turn left into the flea market when you see the stalls. The market covers an enormous area all the way back down to the **Porta Portese** by the Subicio bridge. The fact that so many stalls sell goods – from clothes to household items such as toilet seats – at identical prices suggests that the stallholders are not entirely independent. (From Termini bus 64 to Lago Argentina, then bus 8, which runs along Viale to the distant Trastevere station.)

Above: looking for a bargain at the flea market
Above right: the view from the Acqua Paola

The flea market, which packs up at 1pm, runs parallel to Trastevere to Porta Portese beside the **Sublicio** bridge. This is opposite Capolinea, a tiny bus terminal (buses 56 and 60). This southern section of Trastevere, between the Viale and the river, is the area's up-market neighbourhood and contains several recommended restaurants.

If you can spare the time before eating to see an obscure sculpture by Gianlorenzo Bernini, head up the main street from the Porta Portese towards Viale Tastevere and make a short diversion to your right into the **Piazza San Francesco d'Assisi** to visit the church of the same name. There are a number of interesting paintings here, and in the Albertini chapel, immediately left of the altar, you might want to pay particular attention to a glorious reclining figure, *The Blessed Ludovica Albertoni*. Her saintly face expresses a captivating, mystical ecstasy, and the lifelike hands, typical of Bernini, look as if they are made of silk rather than laboriously fashioned from marble. Another treasure to be admired in this little church is the work above the altar, *The Virgin and Child with St Anne*, by the Genovese artist known as Baciccio (1639–1709) who has been called 'the Bernini of painting'.

Florentine artists are represented across the river, in the church at the top of **Via Giulia**, a picturesque street lined with 16th-century palaces, discreet boutiques and galleries. Near Michelangelo's ivy-covered overhead bridge is a stop for the 116 electric bus, whose route takes in the Campo di Fiori,

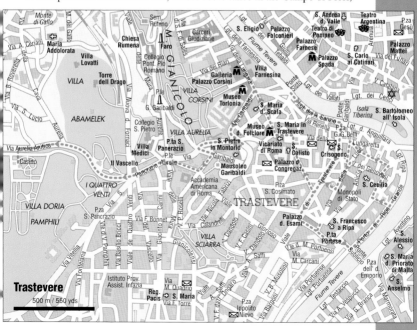

Trastevere

500 m / 550 yds

the Pantheon and Marcus Aurelius's column in the Piazza Colonna. It crosses the Corso within a stone's throw of the Piazza Navona and the Trevi Fountain and terminates beyond the Barberini Metro Station at the foot of Via Veneto. But, for now, let's return to Trastevere.

Start at the Capolinea bus stop (*capolinea* means 'head of the line'), and carefully dodge the cars and motorcycles as you wend your way along Via di San Francesco a Ripa, past San Egidio, to the central square of **Santa Maria in Trastevere.** Here you can sit on the steps of the 300-year-old fountain and admire the church's 12th-century tower and fine mosaics. Even at its busiest, the Piazza Santa Maria is captivating. Children kick footballs and chase pigeons; tourists buy foreign newspapers at the kiosk and photograph each other; students hawk their poetry; and, from the seats of the parked motorcycles, stray cats warily watch the passers-by.

Settimiano Arch

In the adjoining little **Piazza San Egidio**, the **Folklore Museum** has a section devoted to the much-loved 19th-century poet Trilussa, whose life-size statue stands beside the Acqua Paola fountain. The museum has very little to see for the admission charged. Head out of the main square along Via della Scala to the splendid **Settimiano Arch**, attributed to Septimus Severus (emperor AD193–211) and incorporated into the city walls in the 6th century. There's an expensive café beside the arch with outdoor tables from which you can watch the vibrant, ever-changing street scene. Off Via della Lungara, past the arch, through a doorway and up an impressive stairway, is the 15th-century **Palazzo Corsini**, which houses the National Academy and Galleria Corsini (open till 2pm, closed Mon). Painters whose works are displayed here include Rubens, Caravaggio and Van Dyck.

In 1883, the palace gardens became the **Botanical Gardens** (closed at sunset). These beautiful gardens feature several tinkling waterfalls, thousands of different plant species, a scented garden for the blind and a collection of medicinal herbs. Across the street, the **Villa Farnesina** (Mon–Sat, 9am–1pm), built in 1508 by Baldassare Peruzzi for the Sienese banker Agostino Chigi,

city itineraries

contains Raphael's classic *The Triumph of Galatea*. Much of the villa's gardens, which once stretched to the Tiber, were uprooted in the 19th-century when the river's embankments were constructed, but the interior of the villa is splendidly decorated, especially Peruzzi's **Sala della Prospettiva** with its clever *trompe l'oeil* frescoes. When the villa became the property of the Farnese family in 1580, there was an ambitious plan to link it to the Farnese palace across the Tiber but it came to nothing.

The route along Lungara leads to the Vatican but we will go back through the Arch of Settimiano, and up the hill along **Via Garibaldi**, to visit the Gianicolo, the hill on which, in the 7th century BC, Tarquinius, the Etruscan leader, is said to have been standing when an eagle flew down to perch on his shoulder. He took it as a portent that he would rule Rome, which turned out to be the case.

Fontana Paola

Climb the wide steps to the **Piazza San Pietro in Montorio**. In the precincts is Bernini's circular *Tempietto*. Continue beyond the Spanish Academy and up to the fabulous **Fontana Paola**. This fountain was erected in 1611 by Pope Paul, who restored Trajan's aqueduct that brought water from Lake Bracciano in the north. The No 41 bus (from G Carini) turns right here, past the ugly Fascist-era monument and busts of military heroes to the majestic statue of **Giuseppe Garibaldi** (1807–82). The snack bar here is well-placed for a fine view of the city. Heading back along Pancrazio, just before passing through the immense walls built by the emperor Aurelius, look for an old building bearing the name Michelangelo; today, sadly, it is merely a facade concealing water pipes. A little way down Via Giacomo Medici is the grandiose **American Academy**, which insists upon a letter of introduction before granting admission.

Keep left, heading downhill, to return to the main piazza. If there's time, take a stroll in the city's largest and most peaceful park, in the grounds of the **Villa Pamphili** behind the Gianicolo. (Walk from the arch along Via Aurelia Antica.) Pope Innocent X's nephew, Camillo Pamphili, laid out the lovely grounds and in 1652 built the villa, now a museum. The park has many exotic trees and a fountain originally designed for the Piazza Navona by Bernini.

Left: the Gianicolo. **Above**: Trastevere's Santa Maria **Right**: Palazzo Corsini

4. THE VATICAN *(see map, p37)*

Spend a morning in the Vatican museums, visit the inimitable Sistine Chapel, then take in St Peter's Square and the basilica.

Go early to the Vatican museums (open 8.45am–3.45pm).

The 1929 Lateran Treaty was marked by the construction of the **Via della Conciliazione**, a majestic, tree-lined (and traffic-jammed) boulevard that connects St Peter's Square to the forbidding Castel Sant' Angelo. A state within a state, the Vatican, which owns one of the world's largest libraries, has open but well-guarded borders. The gates close at 11pm. Only about one in five of its residents has a car so it's roads are largely traffic-free. The Vatican accredits ambassadors and legations from virtually every country in the world but has no room to accommodate them within its walls.

If you plan to head straight for the museums from other parts of town, the

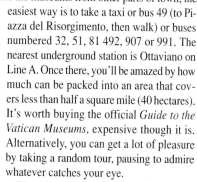

easiest way is to take a taxi or bus 49 (to Piazza del Risorgimento, then walk) or buses numbered 32, 51, 81 492, 907 or 991. The nearest underground station is Ottaviano on Line A. Once there, you'll be amazed by how much can be packed into an area that covers less than half a square mile (40 hectares). It's worth buying the official *Guide to the Vatican Museums,* expensive though it is. Alternatively, you can get a lot of pleasure by taking a random tour, pausing to admire whatever catches your eye.

The 18th-century **spiral staircase** (by Giuseppe Momo) is a phenomenal construction, as you'll realise if you stand at the

Above: St Peter's Square
Left: Momo's spiral staircase

city itineraries

top for a few moments and note that people coming up never meet those going down. Possibly the most famous work of antiquity in the Vatican is the marble **Laocoon** statue, in the **Pio-Clemente Museum**. A 1st-century copy by a trio of Rhodes sculptors of a bronze sculpture dating back to the 3rd century BC, it was noted by Pliny the Elder (who died when Pompeii was wiped out by Mount Vesuvius's volcanic eruption in AD79). Thereafter it was lost until it turned up again in 1506, when it was acquired by Pope Julius II.

'The Highest Ideal of Art'

The statue illustrates the tale told by Virgil in *The Aeneid* of the Trojan priest of Apollo who tried to warn his companions at Troy about the wooden horse in which the Greeks were about to infiltrate the city. The goddess Athene angrily sent serpents to kill Laocoon. This museum also has a fine collection of early Roman statuary, including *Apoxyomenos*. Though it was originally sculpted in bronze in the 3rd century BC by Lysippus, this is a 1st-century AD copy. Lysippus, who also cast Alexander the Great, specialised in capturing the fleeting moment. Here he movingly portrays the fatigue of an athlete after the big race has ended. The athlete is mopping his brow; the title is derived from the Greek word *apoxyein* ('to wipe off').

There's also a statue of Hermes, messenger of the Olympian gods, which was found near Castel Sant' Angelo. And you should see a Roman copy in marble of a 4th-century BC Greek bronze, probably by Leochares, known as the *Apollo Belvedere*, which once stood in the ancient agora in Athens. It's worth noting that the German archaeologist Johann Joachim Winckelmann said of this work: 'of all the works of antiquity that have escaped destruction, the statue of Apollo represents the highest ideal of art.' Before leaving the Pio-Clemente, go through the vestibule to see the wide staircase by Donato Bramante, who also designed the courtyard. The staircase was built at the request of Pope Julius II, who wanted it to be navigable on horseback.

If you're interested in learning about life in the years before the ancient Romans, you should definitely visit the **Etruscan Museum**. The Etruscan civilisation dominated what is now Italy in the five or six centuries before the Roman kings established themselves in the 8th century BC. It's interesting to note that the Etruscans lived in Europe's last matriarchal society.

If you have only the one morning for your visit to the Vatican museums, clearly you must make some choices. You can, if you wish, select from four colour-coded routes, of which A is the shortest at about 90 minutes, and D, for which you will need five hours, the most comprehensive.

The routes incorporate the following exhibits:

A (violet)   classical art, sculptures, tapestries, charts, medieval fabrics, enamels and jewellery

B (beige)   adds Etruscan, Roman, early Christian and ethnological collections

C (green)   plus Egyptian, Roman, Raphael rooms, Fra Angelico frescoes, Borgia apartment with Pinturicchio works, modern sacred art, library

D (yellow)   takes in everything

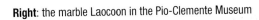

Right: the marble Laocoon in the Pio-Clemente Museum

All routes include the **Sistine Chapel** and its frescoes by the great Michelangelo Buonarroti. Earlier works by Perugino, Pinturicchio, Boticelli and Piero di Cosimo were destroyed to make room for the master's work. Commissioned by Sixtus's nephew, Pope Julius II, Michelangelo worked on the ceiling from 1508 to 1512. Some 20 years and three popes later, Pope Clement VII de' Medici recalled Michelangelo to cover the altar wall with his *Last Judgement*. The 391 figures in this immense work (200 sq m/2,150 sq ft) took three years to complete. If you want detailed explanations of the frescoes, see *The Guide to the Vatican Museums*. View them from different perspectives, particularly from just inside the smaller room.

Michelangelo

Not everybody was happy with the work. A papal aide, Biagio de Cesena, observed that the figures were 'more suitable for an inn', so Michelangelo promptly placed the monsignor along with Charon in the underworld, over which (the pope told him drily) he had no jurisdiction. Leading from the Sistine Chapel is a corridor lined with eye-catching old Latin and Greek gravestones ('To the very sweet pupil of mine, Aphelia', reads one) and more statues: the 1st-century poet Sallustius, a doctor holding a caduceus and numerous two-headed busts of Janus, the ancient Roman deity who guarded gateways.

Take a break in the spacious, formal couryard, with its centrepiece of the golden sculpture *Sphera con Sphera* (1990) by Arnaedo Pomodoro, and a colossal head of Augustus. Resume your tour in the **Pinacoteca**, which features a wealth of religious art spanning the 11th to 19th centuries. Some of the bigger frescoes, the cartoons of their time,

Above: Detail from Michelangelo's Sistine Chapel ceiling
Left: the crux of Christianity

depict biblical scenes. These were installed in small, rural churches to educate the peasants. Note the (badly-lit) Leonardo da Vinci portrait of *St Jerome* in room X; Guido Reni's *The Crucifixion of St Peter* – all light and emotion – in room XIII; and the most famous picture in the collection, *Deposition* by Caravaggio, which is also reproduced in the lobby.

A bus runs from the museums to St Peter's but you can also get there by walking along **Viale Vaticano** beside the towering walls. The museum bus allows you to see some of the grounds, including the **Chinese Pavilion**, the **Papal Academy of Science** and the **Eagle Fountain**, where the water from the Acqua Paola acqueduct first reached the Vatican. You'll also pass the remains of the wall built by Pope Leo IV in the 9th century. The Vatican radio station (FM105 for regular news in many languages) has its headquarters here. If you want to take a tour of the Vatican gardens, contact the Vatican Information Office (tel: 06-69894466) to book a place. You will not see are the pope's rarely-used private railway, the heliport, the supermarket or the printing works, from which emerges the daily newspaper *L'Osservatore Romano* and Catholic literature in a vast range of languages.

St Peter's Basilica

In the 15th century Donato Bramante, at the invitation of Pope Julius II, was the first of a string of architects who began planning a new church, but it was almost a century and a half before building was completed. The original church on the site was built by the emperor Constantine (*circa* AD333) as a pilgrimage shrine over the tomb of St Peter, the martyred first pope.

Today **St Peter's Basilica** and the immense circular piazza over which it presides are awe-inspiring. Michelangelo designed the magnificent dome, which, after his death in 1514, was finished according to his plans. The enormous **piazza** was designed in the 1650s by Bernini. It is surrounded

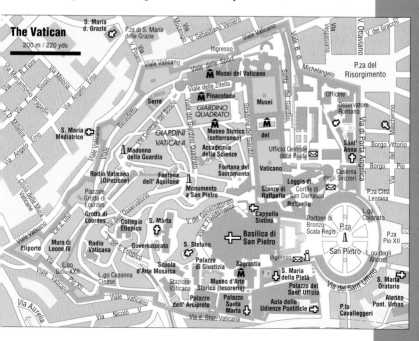

by 284 gigantic columns in four rows, the passage between them so arranged that, viewed from a central spot, the colonnades appear to be a solitary row; a perfect fusion of art and mathematics. An Egyptian **obelisk**, said to have taken 900 men to raise, is the piazza's central feature. It once stood on the spot where Christians were martyred, and was later placed in Nero's circus. Bernini carved the statue on the left and his pupils were responsible for the 140 statues on the balustrade plus the 13 that crown the basilica. Carlo Maderna designed the facade and one of the fountains. The pope makes an appearance at one of the fourth-floor windows of his living quarters (on the right) every Sunday at noon. He blesses the faithful in St Peter's at 11am on Wednesday mornings in winter; in the vast piazza on Wednesday afternoons during the rest of the year.

The basilica's interior culminates in Bernini's immense *baldacchino* (canopy) in front of the altar, above which a dove glows from the natural light of a golden window. The 119-m (390-ft) high **dome** by Michelangelo and Bramante can be reached via stairs or a lift (open until 4.45pm in winter, 6.15pm in summer; admission charge). Bernini's elaborate monument to Pope Urban VIII is by the altar; his last work, a monument to Pope Alexander VII (completed in 1678), is on the left, and his statue of Constantine the Great is in the portico. Cornacchini's statue of Charlemagne is on the right.

La Pietà

The most important work in the church is Michelangelo's exquisite *La Pietà*, just right of the entrance. The signature on the Virgin's sash is the only one on any of Michelangelo's works and is said to have been surreptitiously carved by the artist after the statue's installation when word reached him that it was being attributed to someone else. Since the attack by a hammer-wielding maniac in 1972, *La Pietà* has been protected by bulletproof glass.

Although it's almost always full of people, the spacious basilica only seems crowded during Mass. (The aisles at each side are 76m/250ft in length.) Occasionally, the throng parts to allow the passage of a platoon of Swiss Guards, recognisable by their distinctive orange-trimmed blue uniforms.

The subterranean **grottoes** (entrance near the statue of St Peter by the canopy) hold the tombs of early popes, including one believed to be that of St Peter. The Vatican is linked to Castel Sant, Angelo by a passageway, Passetto di Borgo (built as an emergency escape route) which is due to be opened to the public.

Above: view from the dome of St Peter's
Right: Michelangelo's *La Pietà*

5. THE SPINE OF ROME *(see map, p18–19)*

Take a stroll along the lively, bustling Via del Corso, from the pretty churches of Piazza del Popolo to the famous palaces of Piazza Colonna.

The spine of Rome is formed by the broad boulevard of the **Via del Corso**, running from Piazza del Popolo to Piazza Venezia. It's a promenading street that seems built for people-watching and window-shopping. This is the place where romantic youngsters go to eye each other up, and where venerable seniors find examples of the decline of conventional mores.

Piazza del Popolo has two lovely churches, one on each side of the Corso, and two famous cafés. On the left, the classy but understated **Canova** is a café for conventional types. On the other side of the street, the elegant but somewhat bohemian **Rosati** represents the *dolce vita* (sweet life) enjoyed by Rome in the late 1950s and early '60s. Here was the pick-up place where real and fake movie directors, producers, stars and starlets would gather in the late afternoon, before moving to Via Veneto for the rest of the night. Big hotels, empty bars and two newspaper vendors that stay open late are about all that's left of Via Veneto's glory. Rosati retains rather more of the *dolce vita* aura, and you can still eat at the **Bolognese** next door.

Pope Alexander VI

If your tastes incline more towards the classical, the Renaissance church of **Santa Maria del Popolo** features Pinturicchio's glorious *Birth of Christ*, two dramatic Caravaggios, Raphael's Cappella Chigi, Del Piombo's *Birth of Mary* over the altar, a Lorenzetti *Jonah and the Whale* sketched by Raphael and two Bernini sculptures. Check out the tomb of Pope Alexander VI (aka Cardinal Borgia), whose lover Vannozza Catanei bore him four children.

Alexander VI, elected pope in 1492, was the arch enemy of Martin Luther. In 1510 the German reformer travelled to Rome to fight what he saw as the Church's degeneration and debauchery. He stayed at the Augustinian convent attached to Santa Maria, where he held Mass. Afterwards the pope removed the altar and, rumour has it, Luther's cell was turned into a toilet.

The three main streets leading from the Piazza del Popolo are known as

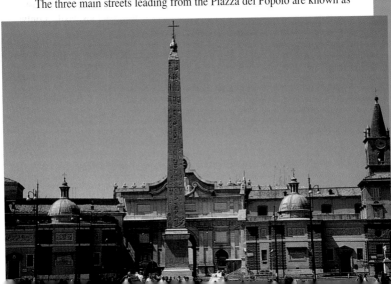

the *tridente*. The central one is the Corso. With your back to the Aurelian walls at the piazza's north end, go down **Via di Ripetta**, the street on the right. Soon you'll see some graffiti, the work of students from the Roman Academy of Painting. The students take much of the credit for making the area so lively. Next is a quiet and appropriately funereal grave mound with the urns of emperors Augustus, Tiberius, Claudius and Nerva encircled by cypresses. Nearby, on the other side of the road, the **Ara Pacis** (Tues–Sat 9am–1.30pm) is a strange, ugly, squat building encased in glass. This is the altar to the Augustan peace that began in 13BC and continued for several decades after the emperor's death in AD14, giving to the Roman empire, and indeed the world, the only century without major wars to date.

Return to the Corso and soon, on your right after the fashionable Via dei Condotti, you'll arrive at the **Piazza Colonna**, which is recognisable by its 30-m (98-ft) high column of Marcus Aurelius. This emperor, who ruled for 19 years, is noted for his appreciation of Greek cultur. The column is decorated with reliefs of the emperor's foreign campaigns, but 5m (15ft) of its base are buried underground. Today the column is topped with a statue of St Paul. The square is flanked by palaces. The **Palazzo Chigi** was built by a Sienese banker, and the **Palazzo Wedekind** has 16 magnificent pillars.

Adjoining the Piazza Colonna with its Galleria Colonna – the city's only major glass-covered gallery – is the **Piazza Montecitorio**. This square is known throughout the country because the *Parlamento* is housed in the Palazzo Montecitorio. Bernini drew up the plans for this building in 1650 and Carlo Fontana saw the design and construction through to completion in 1697. Virtually all that remains of the 17th-century design is the convex curve of the facade, created to make the palazzo look even bigger than it is, and the rusticated columns. The Egyptian obelisk in front of the palazzo was used by Augustus for an enormous sundial, which was discovered in the crypt of the nearby church of San Lorenzo in Lucina.

Saving the Corso

Two temples to mass Italian fashion face each other on the Corso: La Rinascente (four floors) for adults and Babilonia (on the hectic ground floor) for youth. The feeling among Romans is that, these two establishments notwithstanding, the clothes shops overflowing from the Corso are tacky. There's talk about saving the Corso from too much commercialisation, and of restoring the most elegant 19th-century buildings. But until that happens, the area's elegance is confined to the three streets that lead off the Corso to Piazza di Spagna.

Previous Page: Piazza del Popolo
Left: Ara Pacis

city itineraries

6. POPES AND HERETICS *(see map, p18–19)*

Take a half-day tour of Castel Sant' Angelo, Piazza Farnese, and Campo dei Fiori.

The emperor-philosopher Hadrian (AD 76–138) designed his own mausoleum beside the River Tiber in what is now central Rome. Today it is the **Castel Sant' Angelo** (daily 9am–8pm, closed Mon). The mausoleum was the start of a vast construction that became part of Aurelian's walls, then a fortified citadel to defend Rome during the dark ages when the city was at the mercy of northern marauders. Pope Gregory the Great named the citadel Castel Sant' Angelo in 590 after a vision of an angel heralded the end of a plague in the city.

When France's Charles VIII invaded Rome in 1494, the city's defenders repelled him with arrows and missiles fired from the castle. Alexander VI, the Borgia pope, and hundreds of people survived in the besieged castle. Pope Clement VII took refuge there in 1527 while the Constable of Bourbon's troops ransacked Rome. The pope watched helplessly as the city was engulfed by flames. But the castle held out, and the pope remained safe. A passageway built in 1277 to link the castle to the Vatican palaces can still be seen, a block away from the Via della Conciliazione.

The best approach to the castle is from its own bridge, **Ponte Sant' Angelo**, the most spectacular of all the city's bridges over the Tiber. Built by Hadrian, it survived 15 centuries until collapsing in 1450 under the strain of masses of pilgrims celebrating a holy year. It was duly rebuilt, incorporating the ruins, and in the 17th century Bernini and his pupils sculpted the figures of angels that still grace it today. The gigantic Archangel Michael, his sword at the ready, is a later work by an 18th-century Flemish sculptor, Pieter Wershaffelt.

The graceful but imposing Castel Sant' Angelo houses

Above: Castel Sant' Angelo, on the far side of the bridge
Right: the bronze angel outside the Castel Sant' Angelo

artefacts from all periods of Roman history, including the Chamber of the Urns, which contains the ashes of Hadrian's family. (Hadrian himself was buried in his beloved villa at Tivoli, in the hills south of Rome.)

You should be sure to visit Castel Sant' Angelo if you're accompanied by teenage children: they'll be captivated by the dungeons, the cannons and piles of cannonballs, and the small but fascinating museum of arms. The café's splendid view of Rome is a rare feature in a city that often considers its monuments too serious to be made comfortable.

Renaissance Rome's First Main Street

Via Giulia, the 16th-century thoroughfare built by Donato Bramante for Pope Julius II, is lined with *palazzi*, churches and antique shops, beginning with the Florentine-style church of **San Giovanni dei Fiorentini** (containing the tomb of Borromini, who designed the altar). To construct this, the first main street of Renaissance Rome, the builders sliced through a jumble of narrow medieval streets, some of which run off Via Giulia itself. In July the street is lit by hundreds of oil lamps and the courtyards and cloisters host classical concerts. Even if you're not a music lover, you should see this exquisite, romantic setting at this time. (Exact dates vary from year to year.)

A lovely archway – a Michelangelo project that was never completed due to lack of funds – spans the lower end of the street. He originally planned to link Palazzo Farnese and its gardens with the Villa Farnesina on the other side of the Tiber (an extravagant concept that says much about Michelangelo and Renaissance patrons such as the Farnese, Borgia and Borghese families). Instead, we're left with this romantic, ivy-covered archway and the curious **Fontana del Mascherone**. This ancient Roman mask, to which a granite basin was added, was fused with the baroque fountain on the right – a rare example of two period pieces combining to form a third. Nearby are the **Palazzo Falconieri** and, with its faded fresco facade, the **Palazzo Ricci**.

Turn left off Via Giulia to arrive in the enchanting **Piazza Farnese**, with

Above: the sun shines on Rome's ochre-coloured rooftops

its two fountains, the Palazzo Farnese, and church linked by a short street to the Campo dei Fiori square. See the two magnificent fountains in Piazza Farnese, which is so big that it is often filled by sunlight all day. The **Palazzo Farnese** (Sun 10am–noon), in which Michelangelo's genius played a major role – the biggest front window is his – is the prototype Renaissance palace. Conceived as an even more magnificent structure, it was scaled down when finished by the young Sangallo. From the square you can see the palace facade but not the courtyard, frescoed salons or the gallery painted by Annibale Carracci. The gallery was given to France for a symbolic 100 lire for services to the pope in the 19th century.

Now to **Campo dei Fiori**, called the field of flowers because at the very beginning of Roman history that is what it was. Markets selling fruit, vegetables and fish have also been here for centuries. In this, one of ancient Rome's liveliest squares, cardinals, fishmongers, pilgrims, vegetable sellers and ladies of disrepute would rub shoulders. This is probably the only square in the city that doesn't have a church. In ancient times, the piazza was surrounded by inns for pilgrims and travellers; since the 17th century it has accommodated their more modern – and often more secular – counterparts. There are still hotels here, which might tempt you if you are romantically inclined. In the time of the Renaissance, some of these hotels were the homes of successful courtesans, the most famous of whom was Vannozza Catanei, mistress of the Borgia pope Alexander VI. On the corner of the square and Via del Pellegrino, you can see her shield, which she had decorated with her own coat of arms and those of her husband and her lover.

Burned at the Stake

With its reputation for being a carnal, pagan place, the square must have seemed a natural spot to hold executions. Of all the unfortunate victims, Giordano Bruno was the most important figure to be burned alive at the stake in the middle of the square. A priest and philosopher, he was accused of heresy and found guilty of free-thinking. He preached a harmonious concept of God and the universe, saying that the Earth is not the centre of the universe but revolves around the sun. The ecclesiastical authorities tried to make him repent; when convinced of his obstinacy, they burned him on a chilly morning in February 1600. Now you can inspect the imposing statue of him, hooded and sombre, with a book in his hands. Today, surrounded by young people and vagrants, travellers and pilgrims of a new kind, it could be said that Bruno still keeps his own people under his wing.

The square has a couple of elegant cafés, several good restaurants and pizzerias, a cinema (with English-language films sometimes screened on Mondays), a good Chinese restaurant (at the start of Via dei Giubbonari), and a chic wine bar that is popular with foreigners and travellers.

Right: flowers at the market

7. A MUSEUM TRIP THROUGH HISTORY *(see map below)*

This tour takes in a few of Rome's 150 museums, travelling from the time of the Etruscans through imperial Roman and on to the 18th century.

If you want to immerse yourself in ancient Rome, head for the museums, where you can feel, smell and touch it. All you'll need are a bit of patience, imagination, and this chapter. It will have to be a fast ride through the centuries as Rome grows from its grim, austere birth as an outlaws' village, to the splendour of Augustan times, when Roman emperors ruled over much of the world, through the adoption of Christianity and the slow demise of the colossal structure that left the door open to barbarian invasions.

Our story begins with the Etruscans, a civilised, peace-loving people whose women lived as freely as the men. Etruscan society was ruled by sorcerer kings who, according to legend, could order lightning, predict the future and change the course of lives. Great builders with a splendid agricultural system, they were firm believers in the afterlife; indeed they left us with necropolises bigger than any of their 12 towns. For almost 1,000 years they ruled in Tuscany and Latium but we know surprisingly little about them. We don't know where they came from, nor can we understand their language. Historians remain mystified by the ease with which Roman upstarts assumed power – the Etruscans could have defeated them and prevailed for at least another century. At the time Rome was just an outlaws' village.

An Etruscan Heritage

The first three Roman kings were Etruscans, a fact not widely known, and the Roman empire's system of government and administration, its masons, gods, agriculture, sewage and roads – all features ascribed to the greatness of Rome – are the results of an Etruscan heritage. Yet when Rome became

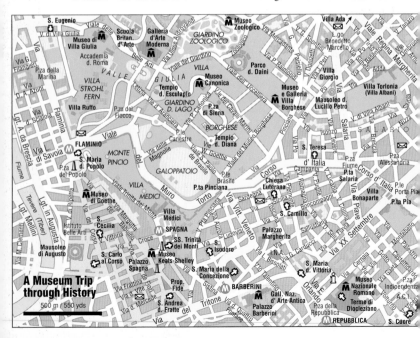

A Museum Trip through History
500 m / 550 yds

strong, one of its earliest priorities was apparently to destroy the Etruscan towns. Only two bronze statues out of the thousands that adorned Etruscan cities are left, but you can see some bronze works in the **Museo di Villa Giulia** (Tues–Sat 9am–7pm, Sun 9am–2pm, closed Mon) at a corner of the elegant Borghese gardens. Here, in the villa of Pope Julius III, the last great Renaissance pope, we begin a tour of Rome's history.

The Etruscans exported bronze throughout the Mediterranean, particularly to Greece (which imported tripods for 15 altars from Etruria) and Egypt. They made wonderful jewellery – their filigree and granular technique was so subtle and sophisticated that only Benvenuto Cellini, the Renaissance master, was able to recreate it. Though the museum is badly presented, the masterpieces speak for themselves. Especially enticing are the *Apollo of Veyo*, whose ineffable smile is an intriguing ancestor of the Gioconda's smile, and *The Couple*, the dignity, tranquillity and vision of whose figures suggest a civilisation unrivalled for depth of emotional feelings. The actual villa was a country retreat rather than a permanent house or *palazzo,* with gardens and pavilions designed by Vignola. Enjoy the quiet beauty of a 16th-century garden while viewing Count Adolfo Cozz's reconstruction of an Etruscan temple, copied from the temple of Alatri.

We move forward in history to Roman times with a visit to the imposing Palazzo Massimo, containing the **Museo Nazionale Romano** (daily 9am–7pm, closed Mon) at Lago Villa Peretti, to the left of the Piazzale dei Cinquecento as you leave the railway station. This is the best introduction to the Roman world. There's a stunning collection of impressive statues, including several masterpieces, on the ground floor, plus an important display of coins and jewels in the basement. The fresco of Livia's house will transport you to that golden era.

Musei Capitolini

Follow this with a visit to the **Piazza del Campidoglio**, designed by Michelangelo and considered to be the heart of Rome past and present. Climb the imposing steps leading to the square to reach the **Musei Capitolini**, which occupy two different buildings (one ticket; free for under-16s and over-60s with ID). Start at the building on the left: enter the courtyard and you will be confronted by a huge reclining sea god and the statue of Marcus Aurelius on his horse, the single most imposing piece of extant ancient Roman statuary. As

Above: Etruscan sculpture in the Villa Giulia
Right: statue of Juno

you climb the stairs you'll see several masterpieces from Rome's golden period. It's no coincidence that the square faces west, towards St Peter's; Michelangelo was in no doubt that the Vatican was the seat of power.

The adjoining **Palazzo dei Conservatori** (*see Itinerary 2, page 25*) served as the seat of the city's magistrates from the late Middle Ages (hence the frescoes) and remains an official building to this day. Recently renovated, it now has shops and a restaurant. It has collected almost as many works of art for display as the Vatican. Here is the single bronze piece, *The She-Wolf*, that links the Etruscans, the Romans and the Renaissance (the twins were added by a Renaissance sculptor in about the 15th century).

The mosaics, frescoes and objects of everyday life, such as lamps, in the **Antiquarium Comunale** (Viale del Parco del Celio 22), demonstrate the craftsmanship of early Rome. The **Palazzo Altemps** (Piazza S Apollinare 44, (behind Piazza Navona) is a new museum that exhibits dozens of statues and an ancient throne never before put on display. Other previously undisplayed Greek and Roman statues can be admired in the dazzling setting of **Art Centre Acea** (Via Ostiense 106). Be warned that this is a bit off the beaten track, in an industrial area set among electrical power generators.

Now we'll continue our race through history with a 10-minute walk (unfortunately through busy 21st-century traffic) away from the Forum and into the Piazza Venezia. From the foot of these steps, you can gaze up at the balcony from which Mussolini would address the crowds.

Egyptian, Greek and Roman Sculpture

Turn left into Corso Vittorio Emanuele II to visit the **Museo Barracco** (9am–7pm), at No 168. This is a compact museum, made up of the founder's personal collection of Egyptian, Greek and Roman sculptures. Here it's possible to trace the links between these three civilisations. Next, walk along Vittorio Emanuele for 550m (601 yards) to **Campo dei Fiori**, the lovely square that sits cheek by jowl with Piazza Farnese, north of the Ponte Sisto. Just behind Campo dei Fiori is the Piazza Capo di Ferro where you'll find the **Galleria Spada** (daily 9am–7pm, Sun 9am–1pm, closed Mon). Here are displayed works by some of the best artists of the 17th century: Rubens (1577–1640) and Caravaggio (1571–1610), Guido Reni (1575–1642) and Guercino (1591–1666), Domenichino (1581–1641) and Brueghel the Elder (*circa* 1525–69). But these works are just the *hors d'oeuvre* to those in the two other magnificent museums.

First is the **Galleria Nazionale d'Arte Antica** (closed Mon), at Palazzo Barberini, Via delle Quattro Fontane 13, a great *palazzo* built by Bernini for one of the leading families. It houses masterpieces from the 13th to the 16th centuries and it has been promising to add 17th- and 18th-century paintings from the Palazzo Corsini, another *palazzo* full of pieces collected through the centuries. With these additions, it will be a gallery of paintings from the important centuries following the dark Middle Ages, when Rome was reduced

to the state of a small village set among the ruins of a glorious past. For century after century during this period, Rome was harassed by invaders. The Castel Sant' Angelo (*also see page 41*) has now been turned into a museum (daily 9am–8pm, closed Mon) containing reminders of the battles of Rome and the exploits of its papal rulers.

Another great family's private collection resides in the **Villa Borghese**, now owned by the state. Following extensive renovations, the Villa Borghese, complete with bar and bookshop, has become the most popular museum in town. Don't miss *Apollo and Daphne* by a young Bernini, and the famous statue of Pauline Borghese by Canova. This work is a fine example of the way Canova captured the beauty and strength of the classical tradition while adding something of his own vision with a polished, almost cold sensuality. When the 19th-century and modern-art galleries are open, you can admire Canova's sculptures, the most modern work so far on this journey through Roman art history. Reservations (tel: 06-32810) are essential.

There are innumerable smaller museums worth visiting. Complete listings, including opening times and a summary of contents can be found in the booklet *Qui Roma* ('Here's Rome'), available free in various languages at the EPT (*Ente Provinciale del Turismo*), Via Parigi 5, near the Termini station, just off the big Piazza Esedra. (The square features a big fountain built in the 19th century by the grandfather of the current mayor, Rutelli.)

Modern Art

With the millennium jubilee have come 20 information kiosks, easily recognised by their octagonal shape. These booths are staffed by multilingual assistants and feature a multitude of maps, leaflets and information about the city's museums and almost everything else of interest to foreign visitors. Contemporary-art lovers will appreciate the recently opened **Galleria Comunale d'Arte Moderna e Contemporanea**, (Via Francesco Crispi 24; Tues–Sat 10am–1.30pm, closed Mon). This being Rome, 'modern' applies to works from the 19th as well as the 20th and 21st centuries.

Another fascinating museum is the **Preistorico Etnografico Luigi Pigorini** (Piazza Marconi 14; Tues–Sat 9am–2pm, Sun 9am–1pm, closed Mon). This museum is located in a somewhat unusual part of town (EUR), where the Fascist architecture of the 1930s still predominates. In addition to the ancient relics – some dating back to prehistoric times – are folk pieces from all over the world. It's good for kids, too.

Left: *The Dying Gaul*
Above: Caravaggio's *Bacchino Malato*

8. BATHS, TOMBS AND THE APPIAN WAY *(see map, p50)*

Morning tour of the Caracalla Baths, the Via Appia and the Catacombs.

Take the 18 bus along the Appian Way.

'Here I can be a man,' was the attitude of the ancient Romans when they went to the baths, the meeting place for everyone from the emperor downwards. The communal baths were a way of life for Rome's upper classes, and there were baths for ordinary citizens too. Wherever the Romans conquered, they built baths which, along with their roads and water and sewage systems, became the mark of Roman civilisation. Reflecting the times in which they were built, they were simple and sensible during the republican era and, by contrast, sophisticated, complex and luxurious in the days of the emperors, becoming decadent towards the end of their rule.

The most popular baths to visit today are the **Baths of Caracalla** (weekdays until 6pm in summer, 3pm in winter) near the edge of the city and enclosed by Aurelian walls. Emperor Caracalla opened them in AD217, after which they functioned for 300 years, with up to 1,500 people bathing at the same time, until destroyed by the Goths. The imposing remains demonstrate ancient bathing procedures in the tepidarium (fairly warm), frigidarium (cold) and sauna. At the entrance is the workout room and then the gymnasium with its patterned mosaic floors. A trip to the baths was not just about bathing; there were Latin and Greek libraries, a lecture room and a chapel dedicated to Mithra, a bloodthirsty god favoured by the army, which exported Mithraworship to the furthest points of the empire.

Above: Tombs of the Scipioni
Left: outside the Catacombs of St Calixtus

There was also a place for swimming, an open-air stadium and a massage room. The Caracalla Baths were richly decorated with beautiful mosaics but few survive. The Farnese family plundered them in the 15th century to decorate their palace near Campo dei Fiori. Today the French embassy is housed at the site of the former baths and the remaining mosaics are well-preserved. In July and August operas are staged at the baths.

From the Caracalla Baths it's a short walk to the **Tombs of the Scipioni**. The Scipioni were a family of generals, of whom Scipio Africanus, as he came to be known, defeated Hannibal at the beginning of the 3rd century BC. Their ashes are in urns in the Columbarium on **Via di Porta San Sebastiano**, a road which takes its name from a gate in the old walls built by Aurelian to defend the city from marauding German tribes. As in other parts of Rome, the walls are immense (12m/40ft high and 3m/12ft thick). There was a time when they stretched for 18km (11 miles), with 381 towers and 18 gates including **San Sebastiano** (originally called Porta Appia but renamed by the Christians to honour the saint's nearby basilica and catacombs). After the Christians defeated the Muslim fleet at Lepanto in 1571, their victorious leader, Marcantonio Colonna, led a triumphant procession from the Appian Way to this gate. Today the towers house a museum (9am–1.30pm, closed Mon) with prints and models illustrating the history of the walls. This is one of the few places where you can actually walk along the walls and see how things were incorporated into them – for example, Cestius's pyramid, the Porta Maggiore arches of the aqueduct to the south-east of the Termini station, and Hadrian's mausoleum.

The Appian Way

The famous **Appian Way** begins here, although if you want to see it vaguely resembling the way it used to be, you'll have to take the 118 bus to the end of the line and begin your walk there. In parts it's still shaded with cypresses and pine trees, and paved with some of the original polygonal cobblestones (*basoli*).

Considering the date it was built – 312BC by Appius Claudius, a city official – the road is a remarkable piece of engineering. Its builders conquered marshes, kept it straight for the first 90km (56 miles) and linked part of it to a parallel canal which allowed travellers to alternate the carriage or horseback trip with a boat ride. The standard width (4.2m/14ft) included pavements and allowed two carriages to pass. Every 10–17km (7–12 miles) were resting places where travellers could change horses or stay overnight. Where the road passed towns it was flanked by great villas and sometimes tombs or other monuments. Extended over the years, the Appian Way reached Brindisi on Italy's southeast coast, almost 640km (400 miles) from Rome.

The wealthy not only lived along the Appian Way – many wanted to be buried here, which explains the presence of so many tombs. These begin outside the city walls (it was forbidden to bury people in the city), notably with the gloomy **Catacombs of San Sebastiano**. Numerous rooms and passages were cut into the soft *tufo* stone of the catacombs. Each room has thousands

Above: detail from Caracalla Baths mosaic

of niches called *loculi,* each with two or three bodies. There are probably 100,000 people buried here. The Crypt of the Popes, where the early popes were buried, and that of St Cecilia are open to the public. The **Catacombs of San Calixtus** join San Sebastiano's, the whole complex taking up four levels (only one may be visited) and stretching for 400m (1,300ft) underground.

Appian Way

500 m / 550 yds

The San Sebastiano tombs were the first to be called catacombs after the Greek *kata kymbas*, meaning 'near the caves'.

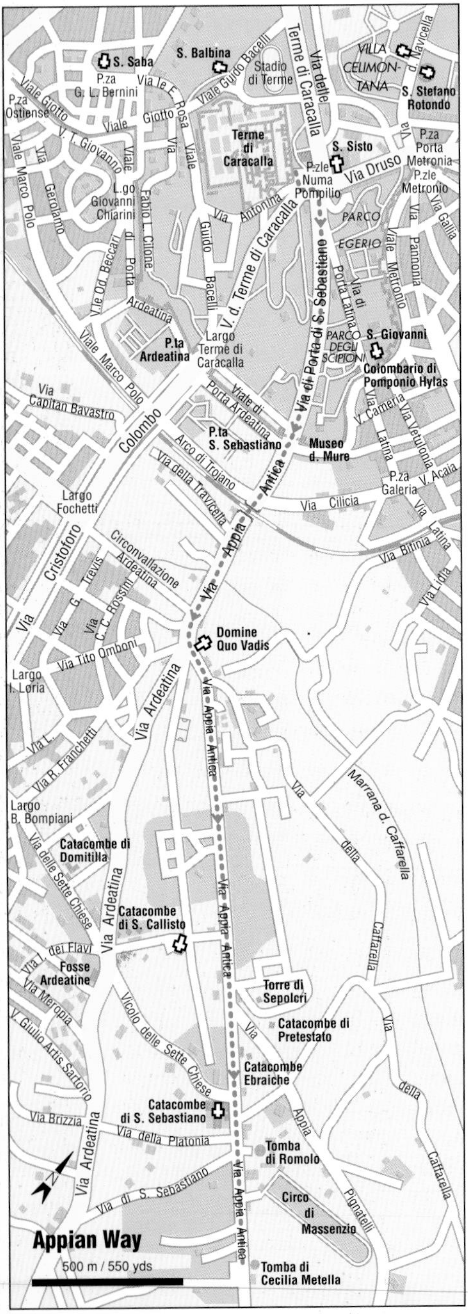

Cecilia Metella

After passing the **Basilica of San Sebastiano,** which is almost opposite the mausoleum of Romulus (son of the 4th-century emperor of that name) in its own little park, you will see a cylindrical tower on the hill on the left. This is the **Tomb of Cecilia Metella**, built in about 50BC for the daughter of Quintus Metellus Creticus (conqueror of Crete). She married Crassus, whose father ruled Rome with Caesar and Pompey for 10 years from 60BC. The fortress-like tomb, decorated with sculpted marble, was put to good use in the 14th century by the upstart Caetari family, relatives of Giotto's patron Pope Boniface VIII, who used to exact tolls from passers-by. The poet Byron wrote about Cecilia Metella in *Childe Harold* but very little is known about her life.

Next to the tomb is the huge (520m/1,700ft by 52m/170ft) **Circo di Massenzio** where 10,000 fans would watch chariot-racing. It's flanked by the ruins of an imperial palace. A nicer part of the Appian Way begins past the **Via Cecilia Metella**, 5km (3 miles) from the city. *La Via Antica Appia*, a free leaflet identifying the area's many tombs, is available from the office of EPT (Ente Provinciale del Turismo) at Via Parigi 11, near Termini station.

9. THE JEWISH QUARTER & TIBER ISLAND
(see map, p18–19)

Visit the exquisite Piazza Mattei, the legendary Portico d'Ottavia and Tiber Island, which has long been associated with healing.

We begin our tour at the **Piazza Mattei**, a lovely small square with the most elegant, delicate and exquisite of fountains in a city full of such beautiful monuments. The Fontana delle Tartarughe (Tortoise fountain) was made by Matteo Landini in 1584. It depicts four graceful, slender boys holding a dolphin on one hand and pushing a tortoise into the upper basin with the other. Even if you get close to those well-sculpted hands, it's difficult to realize that the tortoises were added later, by another sculptor. Opposite the fountain, Palazzo Mattei houses the Emeroteca music academy. From the roof of this public building, you can enjoy a fine view of the Jewish Quarter.

Turn into Piazza Lovatelli and proceed along Via Sant' Angelo in Peschia to reach the **Portico d'Ottavia**. The portico is all that's left of a hall of columns, 118m (388ft) wide by 135m (450ft) deep, erected in 147BC by Metellus to display statues captured from Greece. In some ways this was the very first Roman museum; Augustus dedicated it to his sister Octavia, the abandoned wife of Mark Antony, hence the name.

According to the historian Gregorovius, 'It was here that Vespasianus and Titus led the procession of victory over Israel with ceremonial displays.' The bitter war in Palestine led to a definitive defeat for the Jews, who scattered across the empire. Of the Jews living in Rome, many were originally brought as slaves by Pompey. Latterly appreciated for their financial and medical skills, some went to live across the river in Trastevere while others settled in this neighbourhood. But when the empire converted to Christianity, Jews were branded 'murderers of God' and heretics. In the Middle Ages, by contrast, they enjoyed relative freedom, to the extent that, in Anacletus II, Rome had a pope from a converted Jewish family.

The Ghetto

It was Pope Paul IV Caraffa who, on 26 July 1556, ordered the Jews to be forcibly moved to the area around the Portico d'Ottavia into what was from then on called the ghetto, or 'Jew-pit'. They were permitted to leave the ghetto, which was surrounded by high walls, with doors locked from the outside at night, only if wearing a yellow hat (for men), or a yellow veil (women). Jewish doctors weren't allowed to treat Christian patients and Jews were generally banned from trading with Christians. On Sundays they were made to go to the nearby church of Sant' Angelo in Pescheria and forced to listen to Christian sermons. This continued until 1848.

Right: kosher butcher at Portico

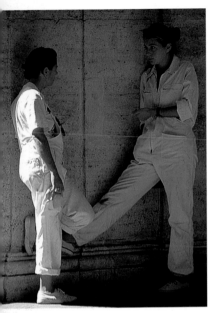

The unification of Italy improved matters, but persecution returned with the outbreak of World War II. The Fascist regime shipped Jews off to Nazi concentration camps, though many well-meaning Italians not only disapproved but actively helped the Jews in any way they could.

There are still many Jews living around here. There are now dozens of kosher-meat butchers and a large synagogue built in 1874 when the new Italian state was conducting fierce political battles with the papacy (ultimately reducing its possessions to what is today the Vatican City). These days the pope enjoys a harmonious relationship with the local Jewish community, and indeed the Vatican has gone some way to establishing mutually respectful ties with international Jewry and with Israel.

Tiber Island

The Jewish Quarter, walled or not, was far too cramped for its inhabitants to live comfortably and, built on marshland, it was none too healthy. It did however benefit from a small but active port facing Tiber Island – the strangely beautiful island that the Romans connected with the mainland, first with a wooden bridge and then a stone one. According to legend, in 293BC the Romans asked the Greeks, their god Asclepius in particular, for help in overcoming a plague. They were sent a ship full of snakes, whose venom was used, alongside dream therapy, to cure major ailments. The plague defeated, the island was dedicated to curing the sick.

The church of **San Bartolomeo** in the island's beautiful central square was built on the ruins of the temple of Asclepius (Aesculapius to the Romans) in the 10th century. The **Ponte Fabricio**, a footbridge connecting the ghetto to the island, was built in 62BC and is still in use, to the extent that cars are also allowed on it today. The other bridge, **Ponte Cestio**, connecting the island to the Trastevere side, is inscribed with the names of the Byzantine emperors who restored it in the fourth century, when they were already strong enough to force their authority on a reluctant Rome. The big medieval tower belonged to the dynasties that used to control the river and indeed the whole area: first the Pierleonis family, then the Caetanis.

The large building with cars parked in its front courtyard is the hospital. The hospital has been situated in the same place, albeit in different shapes and sizes, since that 3rd-century-BC plague. The island is said to resemble the shape of a ship if you look at it from middle distance. And, tucked away somewhere near the down-river end, there apparently exists the sign of the caduceus – the two snakes wrapped around a stick that is the symbol of Asclepius. If you're very fortunate, you might even find it among the lovers who stroll the Tiber's banks on sunny days.

Above: stepping into the shadows
Right: Fontana delle Tartarughe

10. ARTS AND CRAFTS *(see map, p18–19)*

From mosaics and classy windows to pocket sundials and ancient Roman jewellery, this afternoon tour takes in the area south of Piazza di Spagna.

Is a Roman statue a work of art honouring a Renaissance patron, or is it just an anonymous piece of craft? This question continually pops up when you stroll through the quieter streets in the heart of Rome. Art in Rome has always been a means of celebrating power, with examples stretching from the Titus Arch that dominates part of the Forum to the Bernini canopy under Michelangelo's dome in St Peter's. Beyond the expression of imperial potency, art was used to illustrate the civilization's values, including various forms of religious worship and the human will to immortality. These days of course the Roman toga has been supplanted by Biagiotti cashmere sweaters, and Armani jackets. But an aesthetic continuity can be traced from the door-knobs, fountains, statues and buildings of ancient Roman through the Middle Ages, the Renaissance, the baroque era and on to the present day.

Restored Furniture

In **Piazza Farnese**, the elegant **Farnese** showroom displays tiles with motifs first coined in Roman times but which reach into the contemporary, touching all periods of Roman (which often meant Western) arts and crafts. Another place where you can see this historical continuity and the intermingling of art and craft lies along the **Via dei Cappellari**, a narrow, medieval street overflowing with cupboards and cabinets, tables and beds. Here you can watch as craftsmen restore old pieces of furniture. Prices in Cappellari are reasonable and at times even very cheap.

Within walking distance, close to the Sant' Angelo bridge, is **Via dei Coronari**, where the restoration of elegant antiques follow a number of styles. But be warned that Coronari is not cheap and can be dangerously expensive if you fall in love with a piece. The same goes for **Largo Fontanella Borghese**, near which a dozen or more stalls offer everything from the inevitable Piranesi prints and popular depictions of Roman scenery to some dubious but fascinating pieces, and also some neglected but real treasures.

When it comes to gold, there is Cartier in Paris, Tiffany's in New York, Asprey's in London, and in Rome it's **Bulgari.** This is the most exclusive

place in **Via dei Condotti**. If you don't dare venture inside, where an awesome atmosphere reigns, you can peer through the box-like windows that display an array of fabulous jewellery. Bulgari also offers Renaissance pieces, which gives it an advantage over rivals in Paris, London and New York.

In the smart trio of streets leading off the Piazza di Spagna you will find Valentino, Armani, Versace, Laura Biagiotti and Di Donato – another form of art and craft. Don't worry if you don't have a blank chequebook; you only need a nose for culture and a will to appreciate and to understand. Equipped with these attributes, head back to the Farnese area to **Via del Governo Vecchio** and its continuation, Via Banchi Nuovi. In these streets you'll find small but lively, second-hand clothes shops, smart cafés and cheap but stylish shops. The street is full of students and the not-so-young chatting happily and waiting for tables at **Baffetto**.

Interior design is an art form respected by Rome's best museums, in such great *palazzi* as the Borghese or the Pamphili. Indeed what Farnese is to tiles, **Cassius**, at Via del Babuino 100, is to design. Its exhibits present a stark, strong look that calls to mind the work of Le Corbusier. Other showrooms worth visiting for their interior-design works include **Stildomus**, just a few yards away at Via del Babuino 54, and the three-storey **Spazio Sette** in the Palazzo Lazzaroni (Via Barberi 7) near Largo Argentina. This is the place to see a display of practically everything that belongs in a house.

Glass and Ceramics

For glass too, the best place is on Via del Babuino; **Venini**, at No 30, has beautiful shop windows and fine but expensive glass rivalled only in Venice. The most famous name in modern ceramics is **Richard Ginori**, who has a shop at Via Cola di Rienzo 223. For furnishing fabrics, **Cesari** at Via del Babuino 16 is the place to go. If you are looking for wonderful marble, **Franco et Marmiste**, in Via Panico 38–40, offers the best of an ancient Roman tradition. For the equally ancient art of mosaics, check out **Maurizio Grossi** at 109 in the 'painters' beautiful road': Via Margutta.

Above: street art

11. THE SEVEN HILLS *(see p18–19)*

See the sights of the city's famous hills, taking in some panoramic views, ruined temples and magnificent churches and villas.

Most people know that Rome was built on seven hills; they learn it at school along with lessons about a dying Caesar berating Brutus, and Nero fiddling while the city goes up in flames. But in the crowded, traffic-clogged Rome of today, few visitors give the hills a second thought.

There are exceptions, of course. As tourists scramble among the magnificent temple ruins of the Forum, they should be aware of the way it is confined at one side by the gentle **Palatino hill**, on which so many noted republicans had their homes. In times of plague it was a refuge, and its western slope descends towards the Tiber, thus providing access to the sea. The orator Cicero had his home on the Palatino as did the poet Catullus. Augustus was born here and lived simply before building a fine house for his wife Livia. The paranoid emperor Domitian (AD51-96), who was finally assassinated at the instigation of his wife, partially flattened the hill's two peaks to build two large residences. Adjacent to one (the **Domus Augustana**), lies what may have been a stadium built to stage his games.

Other emperors who built homes on the hill where Romulus legendarily founded the city include Nero, Tiberius, Caligula and Septimus Severus, whose arch stands at the northeastern end of the hill. Another access point to the Palatine is from the **Arch of Titus**, built by Domitian to honour his brother, at the other end of the Forum. The palace of Tiberius (AD14-37), the scene of notorious parties, still lies largely unexcavated under the tranquil gardens built by the 16th-century cardinal, Alessandro Farnese. The gardens also hide a tunnel built by Nero; traces of its marble floor remain.

The Capitolino

Adjoining the Palatino is the **Capitolino**, or Campidoglio, the lowest (at 50m/154ft) of the seven hills, which was, and is still the seat of the city's government. Magnificent Michelangelo buildings flank a bronze statue of the the admirable Emperor Marcus Aurelius (AD121-180) among whose maxims was 'our life is what our thoughts make it'. Two of Rome's finest museums are here, filled with secular and religious masterpieces, including works by Tintoretto and Rubens, as well as a statue of the Etruscan she-wolf suckling Romulus and Remus.

On the northeastern side of the Forum, across the Mussolini-built Via dei Fori Imperiale, is the largest of the city's hills, the **Esquiline**, whose northern section (separated by the busy Via Cavour) is called **Viminale** after the forest of bamboo trees (*vimine*) which once covered its slopes. At the apex of the hills stands what some regard as Rome's finest basilica, the 4th-century **Santa Maria Maggiore**. Long before the basilica was built, the poets Virgil and Horace lived on Viminale, as did the wealthy Gaius Marceneas, men-

Right: Farnese Gardens

tor and friend to the emperor Augustus, who had a luxury villa constructed there. Other affluent Romans have favoured the hill over the centuries, many of them building towers (now long-demolished) to boast of their dominance. Unfortunately the Esquiline – most of which is now forms a park centred around its highest point, the Colle Oppio – overlooks one of the city's most dilapidated neighbourhoods, the crowded streets between the slopes and Termini station.

Across the Via Nazionale from Viminale hill, is the **Quirinale**, whose flamboyant palace, Italy's answer to Washington's White House, is the home of the president. The square might appear to be somewhat austere but the maze of surrounding streets is worth exploring. Nearby is the Trevi Fountain and at the other side, near the Piazza della Republica, the **Opera House** and the great **Baths of Diocletian**. Early in the 4th century, these baths were as much a centre of social activity – for hundreds of people at a time – as say the ubiquitous coffee-house chain Starbucks is today.

The Aventino

The Circus Maximus is what separates the Palatino and Capitolino hills from the **Aventino**, a hill that was contained inside the city walls, primarily for strategic purposes, in the third century BC. In the years of the republic, the Aventino was the site of secret meetings and midnight rituals conducted by the sects of Dionysus and Bacchus. These wild, drunken orgies were discovered by the authorities in 186 BC and thousands of participants were put to death. As if to bury forever the hill's history of decadence, Rome's more law-abiding citizens covered it with magnificent temples that adjoined the luxury homes constructed by the aristocracy.

The Aventino earned a reputation as the focus of a peaceful rebellion against the legislature. This disagreement was eventually settled by a senator named Menius Agrippa, who persuasively argued that the people formed

Above: Santa Maria Maggiore

city itineraries

'the arms and legs' of society with the senate being the 'head'. Since then, the Aventino has been synonymous with the idea of dropping out or retiring. The area continued to prosper until 410, when Alaric and the Goths destroyed the hill, leaving it uninhabited. In the following centuries, several churches were built on sacred sites. It is only in recent years that the Aventino has regained its appeal among the smart set.

Today, it is the most residential of hills, covered with churches, including the outstanding **Basilica of Santa Sabina**, set in gardens with fabulous views. Next door is the baroque church of **Santa Alessio** across from the whimsical **Piazza dei Cavalieri di Malta**, designed by Piranesi.

Via Garibaldi

South of the Vatican, the **Gianicolo** is probably the most frequently visited of the seven hills. It is accessible both on foot and by a wide, curving road which, like the piazza at the top, is named after Garibaldi, the lionised hero of the Risorgimento of 1870, which came to a triumphant conclusion with the unification of Italy. A monument to Giuseppe Garibaldi (1807-82) sits in the piazza, near a statue of his wife, Anita, who is portrayed charging into battle on a horse. The Gianicolo offers what are probably the best views of central Rome and there are almost always people up there day and night, strolling, lovemaking, watching puppet shows or outdoor movies (in summer) or visiting the church of San Pietro in Montorio. The church features works by Vasari, del Piombo and the great Bernini. It's a pleasant, if somewhat steep climb on foot from Trastevere, but the Via Garibaldi passes a magnificent arched fountain commissioned by Pope Paul V in 1612.

Celio, in the neighbourhood southeast of the Colosseum, was incorporated into the city in 7 BC when the vanquished citizens of the rebellious city of Alba lived there. Probably the most beautiful of the seven hills, it was once covered in vineyards. Today its spacious park, which surrounds the **Villa Celimontana,** is a very attractive site for picnics. The park is sprinkled with ancient ruins and some beautiful early medieval churches. A steep, narrow road from the frequently renovated **San Gregorio Magno**, originally built in the 6th century, ascends the hill to the church of **Santi Giovanni e Paolo**, whose 13th-century bell-tower was grafted on to the remains of a Temple of Claudius that stood on this site. The original church here was constructed in the 4th century but the present edifice mainly dates back to the 12th century and the interior, lit by numerous chandeliers, is from the early 18th century.

Above: apse mosaic detail

Excursions

1. TIVOLI'S VILLAS *(see map, p60)*

The Villa d'Este and the ruins of the emperor Hadrian's Villa Adriana are both near the town of Tivoli, one hour's drive from Rome.

COTRAL bus from the Rebibbia stop on Line A of the Metro. Also guided tours (American Express and others).

About 40km (25 miles) east of Rome, in gentle hills near Tivoli, lie two aristocratic playgrounds, the Villa d'Este and the Villa Adriana. Though created 14 centuries apart, the two villas have much in common, not least as wonderful examples of what abundant money and style can produce.

Early into his reign (AD113–138) the emperor Hadrian had already made his mark on the vast Roman empire with impressive public works in many regions and Roman cities, including a majestic arch in Athens and the long wall separating England and Scotland. Both still stand today, as do Rome's Castel Sant' Angelo (intended to be his mausoleum) and the magnificent Pantheon (which replaced Agrippa's earlier structure). So Hadrian turned his attention to creating a suitable retreat for himself away from the capital. As emperor he had the power and resources to build what turned out to be virtually a complete town. Much of Hadrian's 'villa' still stands – the **Villa Adriana** (9am–dusk, closed Mon; admission charge), his greatest monument, is today a UNESCO World Heritage site.

This is the most magnificent country villa of imperial Rome. Even today it exudes an atmosphere of wealth and leisure. In addition to homes, hospitals, stables, barracks and thermal baths, Hadrian also reproduced some of the empire's leading landmarks on the 113-ha (280-acre) grounds. These included Thessaly's Vale of Tempe, and what has been called a recreation of the Egyptian city of Canopus with its statue-lined canal leading to the **Temple of Serapis**. (Note that some of the statues are copies of the Acropolis caryatids in Athens.) On a small hill at this end of the grounds are the **Temple of Apollo** and the rectangular **Torre di Roccabruna**, which could well have been an observatory.

Piranesi to the Rescue

The explicatory signs are rendered less than helpful by their academic jargon, but are redeemed to some extent by engravings by Piranesi, the 18th-century equivalent of a documentary photographer. Piranesi's 2,000 engravings were published as *Views of Rome* in 1750, a book that has been endlessly reprinted.

It can take visitors hours to satisfy their curiosity here as they look up at the massive walls that seem

Left: 16th-century frescoes at Villa d'Este
Right: bust of Neptune at Villa d'Este

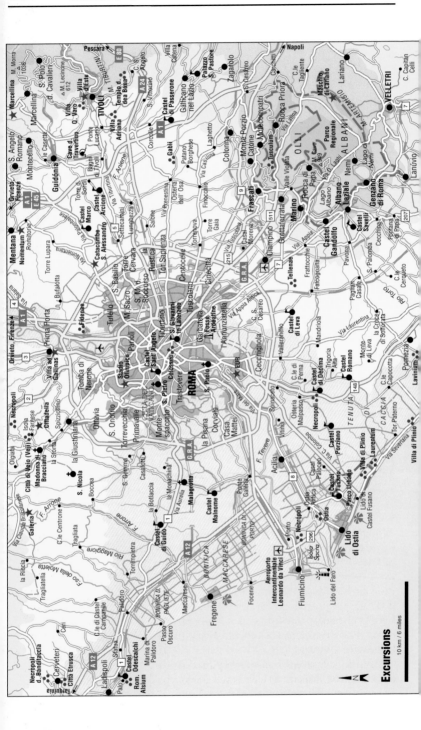

Excursions

10 km / 6 miles

sturdy enough to survive for at least another 2,000 years. The main palace buildings and baths are relatively well preserved, as is the **Maritime Theatre**. This is a circular construction consisting of a portico and a central building surrounded by a canal called the Euripos. This little villa, which was reached by two wooden swing bridges, must have been a perfect retreat for the emperor. For centuries after his death, Hadrian's grand achievement mouldered undisturbed and largely unseen, especially after it was plundered by barbarian invaders. But the Renaissance marked a revival of interest in the ancient sites. Ecclesiastical leaders sought to emulate Hadrian's glory – and they, too, had the money to indulge their extravagant tastes.

Bramante's Vision

Not long after his appointment as pope in 1503, Julius II turned to Donato Bramante for help in creating what became the Villa Belvedere. Since arriving in Rome at the age of 65, the Urbino-born Bramante had spent four years (according to the diarist Giorgio Vasari) 'studiously measuring' the Villa Adriana and was by now considered an authority on the classical style. The design he produced for Pope Julius at the Vatican was said to have introduced 'a new concept of space and dominated the future course of garden architecture'. He died in 1514, his work at the Villa Belvedere still unfinished, but an able successor, Pirro Ligorio, was on hand to complete it. Ligorio (1500–83) was also familiar with the Villa Adriana – he had compiled a portfolio of drawings of ancient sites – and was by then well-schooled in the Bramante style. He especially admired the way Bramante dramatised the steep terrain with monumental ramps and stairs. Thus in 1551, when he was commissioned to build a villa for Cardinal Ippolito d'Este, papal governor of Tivoli, Bramante's vision was much on his mind.

The **Villa d'Este** (9.30am–dusk, closed Mon) was originally a Benedictine convent and today its cypress-filled terraced gardens are indeed a dramatic sight: hundreds of fountains gush from grottoes, statues and rocky clefts, all subtly arranged so that whichever way one turns there is always more water around the corner. The composer Liszt named one of his works after the fountains (one of which, the *Fontana dell' Organo Idraulico*, did play music in its early years). Another of the fountains was designed by Bernini, but even his work is surpassed by the vista of the **Avenue of a Hundred Fountains** on the terrace below it.

Traversing the gardens involves a steep descent and a climb back up, but as long as you aim to conclude your visit well before sunset, you can move at a leisurely pace. You might want to take advantage of the bar and restaurant on the terrace, although prices are higher than in Tivoli itself.

Above: entrance, Villa d'Este
Right: rear view at Tivoli

2. THE ETRUSCAN TRAIL *(see map, p60)*

To the northwest of Rome to the former Etruscan towns of Cerveteri and Tarquinia and the 2,300-year-old bridge at Vulci.

Railway stations: Cerveteri and Tarquinia on the Rome-to-Pisa line; bus: COTRAL, departing from Lepanto (Line A). Vulci is accessible only by car plus a lengthy walk.

This itinerary is highly recommended for romantics, history lovers and, above all, for connoisseurs of mystery and magic. We still know only very little of the Etruscans' origins, and their written code is unique in that it's the only one that modern philologists haven't managed to crack. We do know that they had an efficient agricultural system and were big on fishing. The sophistication of their cooking can be seen on frescoes and basreliefs. According to the Italian book, *Miti, Riti, Magie e Misteri degli Etruschi*, this was a civilisation that knew about its imminent demise but did nothing to prevent it. The same book records other Etruscan paradoxes, such as the way they built cities of the dead that were larger than those of the living, and bizarre beliefs – their sorcerer kings were said to be able to command lightning. (This reputation was so durable that long afterwards – in the 4th century AD, when the barbarians were at the gates of Rome – their assistance was still being solicited for this purpose.)

Cave-Dwellers

The dozen Etruscan city states were rich, powerful and so secure that, for centuries, they didn't even need walls. The omnipotent but benign sorcerer king was helped by the great aristocratic families who had specific civic duties to slaves and the poor. Music accompanied all types of work, be it hunting, harvesting or cooking. The people lived contentedly in thousands of caves that dot their forested lands in Tuscany and Lazio.

The Etruscans never waged war; how the powerful city of Veio, which had a population of 100,000, an army and theoretically impregnable walls, could be captured by an uncouth, barely-armed band of Romans remains a mys-

tery, even though the conquest took 100 years. Why didn't the Etruscans ask for help from their sister cities? No historian wants to believe that they succumbed to fatalism and acknowledged that their time was up.

The great Etruscan iron mines produced the bronze tripods that were found everywhere in ancient Greece. The large Etruscan fleet ranged far and wide as it transported metal-tool exports east to the Danube, north to France, west to Spain and south to Egypt. Of the many thousands of big, bronze statues that graced Etruscan towns we are left with two; ironically, one is the she-wolf in the Capitol, the figure that celebrates the legendary birth of Rome. The other, called the *Chimera*, sits in a museum at Arezzo in Tuscany, and is a strangely complex hybrid, part-feline, part-serpent.

The majority of the best Etruscan sculpture, much of it salvaged from the four Etruscan towns nearest Rome, is today preserved in the Vatican museums (*see page 35*) and Villa Giulia (*see page 49*). **Veio**, which fell in AD396, has yielded an impressive statue of Apollo, whose knowing, mysterious smile bears some resemblance to that of the Gioconda.

Cerveteri

The town of Caere, now **Cerveteri**, produced the bulk of the pieces in Rome's museums, but there are still examples of pottery and sarcophagi to be seen in Cerveteri's own little museum in a Renaissance palace called **Ruspoli** (9am–4pm in winter, until 7pm in summer, closed Mon; admission free). Caere was a commercial port spread over 71km (44 miles) of coastline. From its three harbours it traded with the Greeks and Carthaginians. COTRAL buses to Cerveteri operate every hour from the Metro stop Lepanto (Line A) on the Via Lepanto. The journey takes about 40 minutes.

From the town's main square get a bus to the **Banditaccia necropolis** on the hill. The tombs here are made of great mounds of earth with carved stone bases, often bearing paintings of hunting and fishing scenes and frequently hinting at all kinds of esoteric, magical forces. The most famous, *tomba dei rilievi*, is protected by a glass screen, but others – such as *tomba dei capitali* and *tomba dei vasi Greci* – are more accessible. Everybody was buried in much the same style as they lived – no two tombs are alike. There are said to be almost 40,000 of them in the area, many as yet uncovered, although the *tombaroli*, illegal grave-diggers, continue their nefarious work.

Another Etruscan centre, **Tarquinia** (90km/56 miles from Rome on the busy Aurelia road, and equally easy to reach by bus from the Lepanto bus

Left: Etruscan tomb at Cerveteri
Above: the 7th-century BC Tomba della Cornice, Cerveteri

station), is a lovely, sleepy medieval town with at least three attractive churches (Santa Maria di Castello, San Francesco and San Pancrazio) and a museum located in the 15th-century *palazzo* of the Vitelleschi family in the centre of town. It closes at 2pm (and all day Mon) so you'll need to make an early start. The most impressive piece is a terracotta relief of a pair of winged horses, but there are also numerous sarcophagi taken from the surrounding region and beautiful frescoes taken from other tombs. (Such removals wouldn't happen these days because current thinking sensibly maintains that a piece of ancient art should remain *in situ* where obviously the work can be better understood and appreciated.) If the museum's top floor happens to be closed, the custodian will unlock it for you on request.

The admission ticket also covers the necropolis, a 15-minute walk from the museum and also closing at 2pm. There are thousands of tombs here, most of

them closed and unexcavated, many behind glass. You'll not want to overlook the *tomba della baccanti* (dancers), the *tomba della caccia e della pesca* (hunting and fishing) or the *tomba del triclinio*, which depicts reclining diners at a feast. The Etruscans ate while lying down, a habit copied by the Romans. Though the Romans thought of their predecessors as decadent, the Etruscans were extremely skilled and competent workers. This is obvious from the state of the countryside, the way the cities were built, and the perfect water and sewage systems – civic achievements all copied by the Romans.

The Road to Vulci

To reach **Vulci**, the least accessible of the old Etruscan settlements, you'll need a car. Take the Via Aurelia road towards Grosseto and watch for the Vulci signpost after passing **Montàlto di Castro**. About 9.5km (6 miles) on you'll see the 11th-century black stone fortress of **Ponte d'Abbadia**, which includes a museum (9am–1pm and 2.30–4pm) housing local relics. To walk to Old Vulci, keep left after the bridge, scramble down the grave-covered hill and cross over the stream. You'll pass the Cuccumella, an Etruscan hill grave that's 150m (492ft) in diameter, and see the foundations of the high tower that once overshadowed it. From Tarquinia it's worth making a trip to **Tuscania**, which has two magnificent cathedrals, one dating from the 13th century.

When you have had enough of driving and sightseeing, you can relax on some of Italy's loveliest beaches near **Alberese**, reached after heading through Orbetello and Talamon.

Above: picnickers enjoy a day out
Right: the famous Nile Mosaic

3. THE CASTELLI ROMANI *(see map, p60)*

An hour's drive southeast of Rome will transport you to the medieval village of Frascati, the pope's summer residence at Castel Gandolfo and the pagan shrine to the goddess Diana at Nemi.

COTRAL buses (59, 55, 51) from Metro station Subaugusta on Line A.

In the Alban Hills southeast of Rome, the group of 13 towns known as the Castelli Romani all grew up around feudal castles. Today they are renowned the world over for their excellent food and wine. **Frascati**, the most famous, is delightful. Though located at least 160km (100 miles) from the sea, the town prompted one early 20th-century writer to observe: 'One cannot help imagining the wash of waves instead of the grassy plain of the Campagna at the end of those coiling streets'.

Autumn, when the grape harvest is in full swing, is the best season to visit, not that there's ever a bad time to patronise the friendly taverns. Many good wine shops can be found along the **Via Regina Margherita**, to which some customers bring their own food. (Tasty pieces of herb-stuffed suckling pig called *porchetta* is a regional favourite.)

Spectacular Fountain

Leaving the bus station, the park of the **Villa Torlonia**, with its panoramic views of the countryside, is just to the right. Even more dramatic is the aspect from the **Villa Aldobrandi**, on the other side of the Via Cicerone. This was built for the nephew of Pope Clement VIII in 1602. As with the family's villa on Via Mazzanino in Rome, only the gardens are open to the public, but their centrepiece is one of the most spectacular of all fountains. The 18th-century English diarist John Evelyn was impressed not only by the fountain fed by a water staircase but by an 'elegant' garden that he felt surpassed 'the most delicious places that my eyes ever beheld.'

Marino, the nearest of the Castelli to Rome, also attracts big crowds during the October grape harvest, partly on account of an old song that tells of the fountains that spill wine. On the slopes of **Rocca Priora** is the Greek Orthodox abbey of **San Nilo**, famous for its wine and the splendid singing

at Sunday morning Mass. Also celebrated for its wine is **Rocca di Papa** – 'the Pope's Rock' – on the northern slopes of of Monte Cavo, the highest peak (949m/3,114ft) of the Alban Hills.

The pope's summer residence is a few kilometres away at **Castel Gandolfo**, above the Lago di Albano, where pontiffs have lived since 1624. This was the site of Alba Longa, the city founded by Aeneas, the reputed father of Romulus and Remus. The volcanic lake, which reaches depths of 170m (558ft), is a popular spot in the summer for boating. Occasional regattas and the proximity of the pope do wonders for the local tourist trade. The lake's overflow is handled by a tunnel 1.4km (almost a mile) long, which was carved out of solid rock in 397BC and still does the job admirably.

The most peaceful of the Castelli villages is **Nemi**, which, in pre-Christian times, was a pagan shrine devoted to Diana, goddess of the hunt. Ruins of the ancient temple can be seen on the slopes between the village and the now polluted lake. In 1930 the lake was drained to recover two huge boats (more than 70m/200ft long and 20m/65ft wide) built by Caligula (emperor AD37–41). The recovery was helpful to historians, but the boats were destroyed during World War II. New replicas were put in the lakeside museum, which has been closed for many years.

Cool Palestrina

If you are driving, **Palestrina** makes for an interesting stop-off on the way back to Rome. An Etruscan town with many ruins, it has been a popular retreat for affluent Romans since the days of the early emperors. Reputedly founded by Telegonos, the son of Odysseus, it was originally called Praeneste. When the 1st-century lyric poet Horace, who had a villa in nearby Tivoli, described it as 'cool', he was presumably referring to the climate. The remains of the shrine of **Fortuna Primigenia**, where the goddess of fortune was worshipped, are impressive. Among her later patrons were members of two patrician Roman families, the Colonnas and the Barberinis, whose palaces were built into part of the temple itself. This is now a museum – the Museo Nazionale Archaeologico Prenestino (closed Mon), on the top floor of which is the extraordinary Nile Mosaic, over 2,000 years old, which shows the Nile valley teeming with life. One of the shrine's main attractions in ancient times was the oracle, mentioned in the writings of Cicero.

The little town, enclosed within the temple's extensive walls, is a mecca for admirers of the local mushroom, *funghi porcini*, which for centuries has been a rare delicacy. In the 17th century the town changed its name to honour its most famous native son Giovanni Perluigi di Palestrina, born here in 1525. Palestrina's distinguished career as a composer included many years as organist and choirmaster at St Peter's in Rome.

Above: Swiss Guard at the Pope's summer residence in Castel Gandolfo

excursions

4. OSTIA ANTICA *(see map, p60)*

Travel to Ostia Antica, Rome's ancient port, via Metro Line A from Piramides station, possibly changing at Magliana to join the Lido di Ostia train (on the same ticket). Once you arrive, cross all the highways, and keep straight ahead.

Your best destination for a short excursion is **Ostia Antica**, which can be reached from Rome in an hour. The old port will keep you fascinated until it closes an hour before sunset. Take food and drink – there is none on site – and enjoy lunch with a fallen marble column as your picnic table.

Ostia Antica is among the best preserved of all ancient Roman cities, largely because it gradually declined from bustling port to rural backwater before being covered by sand and forgotten for centuries. The earliest town wall went up in 335BC with the sea protecting the city at the western side. Sitting at the mouth of the Tiber, it was the first landfall for all the treasures bound for Rome from the far-flung corners of the empire. The shipping business was an especially lucrative one with its importers and exporters, timber merchants and boat-builders, and sail- and rope-makers.

From the earliest days, the large quantities of silt deposited by the river caused a problem for the navy; Augustus moved the naval base down the coast, but Ostia continued to flourish as the port at which grain from Africa was unloaded. After Claudius (emperor AD41–54) and Trajan (emperor AD98–117) dredged the harbour and rebuilt the docks, the port continued to grow steadily and by the late 2nd century its population exceeded 100,000. In the 2nd century a new port was built further up the coast and the lifeblood of Ostia began to ebb away. Its decline was later hastened by pirate raids and malaria from the untended and expanding marshes. After the 4th century it was deserted and forgotten – which is what makes it such a superlative time-trip for today's visitors.

Surviving the Centuries

As you stroll down **Decimanus Maximus**, the main street, it is not hard to visualise the scurrying figures who once thronged this roughly paved thoroughfare, passing in and out of the stores and offices, whose empty shells still line each side. Ancient pillars stand on tavern counters and shelves, and you can see an ancient bakery's stone ovens. A mosaic of a fish indicates what was sold in one store; black-and-white tiles depicting wrestlers identify an athletic academy.

Look out for the discreet bilingual signs that explain the many fascinating artefacts. A large **amphitheatre** with 3,000 seats is virtually intact. Check out the small shrine at the crossroads where the broad high street and the winding road to the river intersect. Temples abound. The biggest are those at ei-

Right: Ostia Antica

ther end of the vast **forum**: the **Capitolium**, which has steps as impressive as those of any 21st-century capital city, and the **Temple of Rome and Augustus**, built by Tiberius. Behind the forum were the big public baths, not far from the well-preserved **Casa di Diana**, a three-storey block of flats which had a fountain in its central courtyard, just around the corner from the bakery.

Cleopatra's Roman Rendezvous

Behind the theatre, the big shippers and traders had their offices in the **Piazza della Corporazione**. There were at least 60 of these offices and it's worth seeing their ancient 'trademarks' and the mosaics depicting scenes of busy city life. The River Tiber ran right by the piazza in those days (it has since slightly changed its course) and it is easy to picture tycoons leaning from their windows on that exciting day in AD45 when Cleopatra's regal barge passed by, heading upriver for a Roman rendezvous with Caesar.

On your way back to the station you will see the **castle**, built in 1483 by Baccio Pontelli and regarded as one of the best examples of Renaissance fortifications. Inside, what was once an apartment for the pope is now a small museum. The frescoes on the main staircase are by Baldassare Peruzzi, who was also responsible for the nearby Sant' Aurea church.

Present-day Ostia has little to interest tourists. Even the beaches are more decorative than useful – the water is too polluted for bathing, though there is the 'secret' nudist beach of Il Buco ('The Hole'), so named because access is via a hole in the fence. Be warned that, if you decide to return from Ostia by train, you will discover that **Lido di Ostia** is a long walk from the station. At least you can take advantage of a well-stocked supermarket on the right of the piazza.

Using data supplied by modern electronic recording instruments, British archaeologists have been uncovering an even bigger site in nearby Portus, which had been virtually ignored until the 1990s.

Above: Ostia's amphitheatre
Right: a classical pose

Leisure Activities

SHOPPING

Piazza di Spagna is one of the city's most admired sights. The **Spanish Steps** (built in 1725) that rise above it lead to the French church of Trinità dei Monti. In the 18th century, beautiful people hoping to find work as artists' models would congregate on the steps, which were named after the Spanish Embassy to the Holy See.

The square joins the three streets that serve as the fashion windows for Italian couture. The stylish **Via del Babuino**, **Via dei Condotti** and **Via Borgognona**, together known as the 'tridente', are very popular with tourists. The proximity of the Spanish Steps enhances their appeal and every shop tries to create a mood that exalts the house style. Most of the brand names – Armani, Gucci, Versace, Bulgari – are global trailblazers. Here in the exquisite heart of a city that once welcomed visitors on a 'Grand Tour', Rome offers itself up to visitors once more – this time in the name of fashion.

The city's major shops include the following illustrious names:

Armani, Via del Babuino 140
In the great Italian tradition of Bernini and Borromimi, Dante and Petrarch and, more recently, Fellini and Antonioni, Armani's name is inextricably linked with that of his great rival and friend Versace, who was tragically murdered on the steps of his Roman-style villa in Miami.

For all their contrasting styles, the two contemporary fashion moguls shared comparable visions. Armani, considered by many to be the last of the country's fashion maestros, has been responsible for dressing the elegantly turned out career man throughout the world for a number of years. His shop is, like a temple of church-like silences and an almost ascetic presentation. Whatever you buy, be it a suit or tie, it will be indisputably Armani, with no need for a label.

Left: for classical tastes
Right: selling modern Italian fashion

Versace, Via Borgognona 29
True to family life Italian-style, Versace's sister Donatella took over both the artistic and financial sides of the famed house on his death. Armani and Versace maintain a significant presence in Rome, although the former's headquarters are located in Milan and Versace is truly international.

Valentino, Via Bocca di Leone 15
In a category all of his own, Valentino is smaller than the big two, but he is couturier to royalty and their modern equivalent, movie stars. His shop – featuring ready-to-wear clothes for women – which also serves as his headquarters, reflects his enduring fame. If you have to ask the price, as the saying goes, you can't afford it.

Laura Biagotti, Via Borgognona 43
Indubitably the queen of cashmere. Under a glass roof that enhances colours, she provides a uniquely feminine touch much desired by women who seek to be classy in a gentle, subdued way.

Fendi, Via Borgognona 39
The Fendi sisters own an empire of shoes, bags and accessories. In Italy Fendi is almost as big a name as its more internationally famous contemporaries.

Gucci, Via Condotti (two shops)
Possibly the world's most famous fashion name with a listing on the New York stock exchange and imitated by sweatshops in Taiwan, and in the back streets of Naples. True to the tradition of the Renaissance, Gucci has embraced many a family squabble, but its style – and profits – are ever-visible.

Beltrasi, Via dei Condotti 19
A true home-grown brand, subdued and with an elegance most appreciated by Italians. The handmade shoes and exquisite leather goods emulate ancient Florentine traditions.

Galassia, Via Frattina 20
Marketed as a 'galaxy of fire' (whatever that means). Here you'll find Gigli, Gaultier and the new Japanese stylists, as well as new English designs. Prices are competitive.

Dolce e Gabbana, Piazza di Spagna 82
This stylist couple were outsiders for a number of years but are now firmly regarded as part of the establishment, and are still extravagant and extroverted.

Max & Co, Via Condotti 46
One shouldn't even raise the subject of prices here in the snobby tridente, but Max is your best bet for both clothes and accessories if you want to survive your shopping spree with anything left in your purse.

Oliver, Via del Babuino 61
The youth-oriented part of the Valentino empire is set in leisurely surroundings. Here the unmistakable Valentino style emphasises off-the-shoulder cocktail dresses and evening wear.

Bulgari, Via Condotti 10
If you fancy a $5,000 or $10,000 watch, this is the place to get it. Even the most inexpensive – as opposed to cheap – items within the stark portals of this, Italy's most renowned jeweller, stand out.

Class and tradition are so entrenched in this area that, when a big international maker of jeans tried to set up shop – with the help of a garish neon sign – it caused such outrage that the necessary permits were refused until strict 'aesthetic' standards were met. In the end, the jeans manufacturer gave up and decided to find premises elsewhere instead.

While shopping in this neighbourhood you should visit Antico Caffè Greco, where, in the 19th century, everybody who was anybody went to be seen. Goethe was among the first in a long succession of artists, composers and writers, which continues to the present day. The café remains an elegant, if somewhat stilted, place.

Aside from the 'tridente', the two more conventional shopping streets are Via del Corso and Via dei Banchi Vecchi, which is near Campo dei Fiori. Adjacent to the 'tridente', **Via del Corso** offers such delights as the Rinascente, a four-storey Art Nouveau department store practically in front of Parliament House. Its ground floors are devoted to perfume and other body enhancers, with clothes on the upper floors. Virtually any discerning foreigner will want to visit the Rinascente, next to which is the reputable Babilonia, a great shop for children's wear. Aside from these classic stores, almost the entire length of Via del Corso, from Piazza di Spagna to Piazza Venezia – the spine of the city – is dotted with enough clothes stores to engage a window-shopper for hours.

Via dei Banchi Vecchi, between the Campo and Piazza Navona, lies in the very heart of the old town, whose medieval streets are well worth walking on their own merits. Its good-quality second-hand stores have become trendsetters, especially for the young at heart. Young stylists open up here, often remaining for years before migrating to the 'tridente'. Among the many stores worth checking out here are l'una e l'altra for distinctive women's clothes. For really cheap but classy men's and women's wear, as well s shoes, check out **Via dei Giubbonari**, ust off the Campo, entering the street in the ewish ghetto across the tramway lines.

Art and Antiques

f you are looking for art, **Via Margutta** is a lovely, peaceful street just off Piazza di pagna (though less avant-garde than the rt scene in the Trastevere area). In spite of ecoming over-popular with tourists, it man-ges to retain a lot of style. But can you re-lly do the ultimate? That is, walk into a hop and buy a painting by a master. Even a minor master. The answer is yes, if you an afford it. If you have knowledge, culture nd taste – better still, that indefinable mix-ure of all three that Italians call 'gusto' – you ight be able to find a small masterpiece or a relatively small sum.

Around the corner in Via del Babuino 32–4, W Apolloni is a respected dealer, ith 17th-century paintings, silver, and fur-iture. A few paces away at No 67, Cesare ampronti is the dealer to see for 16th- to 8th-century painters. Also worth checking ut is what Italians call 'Gab' (Granmer-ato Antiquario Babuino), at Via del Babuino 50, for silver, porcelain or glass from the 7th century onwards.

If these shops on Via del Babuino are too xpensive for your pocket, there are other ptions. In spring and at Christmas Via Iargutta holds seasonal fairs featuring af-ordable items. Or you might go to **Via del ellegrino** and **Via dei Coronari**, where, ith a bit of luck, you might end up in a rift shop that has a small Titian, a forgot-n Reni, or conceivably even a Caravag-io. It has been known to happen.

ookshops

ou might also want to check out the book-op Libreria del Viaggiarore in the middle f Via del Pellegrino itself. For other inter-sting bookshops, the Feltrinelli in nearby iazza Argentina offers a good choice of alian-language volumes and also has some English.

For the best choice of English books you ould go to **Via della Vite**, where there are vo stores, one of which is the American ookstore. You could also pay a visit to the on's bookshop at Via del Babuino 181, or the Economy Book and Video Centre in Via Torino 136, which, as its name indicates, sells videos as well.

Markets

Don't overlook the shopping area around the **Piazza Vittorio Emanuele II**, which has recently become a fledgling flea mar-ket, with scores of stores run by immigrants, mostly from East Asian and African coun-tries, and a good choice of inexpensive eater-ies. The area between Piazza Vittorrio and Termini Station is particularly fun to explore. For exotic items go to the Mas department store which, if it has survived a long-stand-ing threat of closure, is probably the cheap-est such outlet in all of Rome.

The Piazza Vittorio morning market has also been scheduled to close for some time, which is a shame because it has an atmo-sphere to savour. If it's still open, pay a visit at any time before 2pm.

Another colourful morning market, the **Mercado di Testaccio** in the piazza of that name, concentrates on food – mostly fruit and vegetables. And there's a small market every morning in **Campo de' Fiori**.

If you can't make it to the Sunday mar-ket of **Porta Portese** (*see page 30*) with its assembly of everything from caviare to 1930s editions of the *New York Sunday News* comic section, you should visit the daily clothing market in Via Sannio. Every morn-ing, along a stretch of the Aurelian walls near the S Giovanni Metro station, huge stacks of used clothes, shoes and camping gear are piled high in stalls arranged along narrow, bazaar-like corridors. Patient ex-ploration should result in real bargains.

bove: you never know what you'll find in Rome's markets

EATING OUT

Pizzerias and Trattorias

Romans call them *pizza al taglio*. They are small, colourful places found everywhere in the city, with hot pizzas served in rectangular shapes of any size you want – you pay according to weight. Sometimes there are tables in these places, but not often, for most customers wolf the food down while standing. Pizza parlours, where you sit down, serve the familiar big, round pizzas with a wide and sometimes wild range of toppings: tomatoes, potatoes, aubergines and their flowers, zucchini and almost any other vegetable you can think of, as well as various meats, ham and fish. White wine is the best companion to Roman pizza, but a glass of beer accompanies it well too.

Trattorias serve heavy Roman food: lots of oil and meat with rich sauces. For starters, your pasta might be long (*spaghetti*) or short (*rigatoni, pasta corta, bucatini*); your sauce could be *aglio e olio* (oil and garlic – the simplest), *amatriciana* (spicy tomato sauce and bacon) or *carbonara* (bacon, egg yolk, pepper and Parmesan or pecorino cheese). Try *penne all' arrabiata*, a short kind of pasta with strong *peperoncino* making it very hot.

Your main course will be meat or fish. In addition to beef-steak and pork-chop options, there is what has traditionally been the fare of the less affluent – cheaper cuts of meat and offal, such as *trippa* (tripe), *cervello* (brains), *rognoncino* (sliced kidneys), *agnello* (lamb) and *abbacchio* (mutton), with assorted sauces. A classic trattoria dish is *saltimbocca alla romana* (a slice of prosciutto ham and a leaf of fresh sage rolled up with a thin slice of veal, then browned in butter and simmered in white wine).

Around Piazza di Spagna, the nameless place at Via Margutta 82 serves good-quality food for $15–27 (£10–18) in an expensive part of town. At the corner of Corso and Via Condotti, at Via del Leoncino 28, is the **Pizzeria Il Leoncino** (tel: 06-687 6306) where you can get a good pizza meal for about $10 (£7) including wine. If, for whatever reason, you are inclined to plunge into the world of Italian journalists and politicians, you'll frequently find members of their number dining at **Gino** (Vicolo Rossini 4, tel: 06-6873434) where you can enjoy a tasty meal for around $15–18 (£10–12). It's located between the Pantheon and the Parliament.

At Piazza Pasquino 73, the **Cul de Sac** (tel: 06-68801094) is a wine bar that displays hundreds of labels collected over the years. Light meals here start at around $15 (£10). Nearby, still in the Piazza Navona area, is Baffetto (Governo Vecchio 11). Baffetto is particularly popular among students, but is perhaps the victim of its own fame. Pizzas here are good as well as cheap, and you can watch the world go by from an outdoor table while you dine.

Further down the road, the street changes its name, becoming Via Banchi Nuovi. At **No 14** is a small trattoria that has been run by an elderly couple, known as Alfred and Ada, who have been serving up delicious meals (by all accounts) for more than half a century. You eat what's offered – there's no choice of menu, just as it was in the pre-*dolce vita* 1950s: a $22 (£15) trip into Rome trattoria of yesteryear.

Campo dei Fiori's **Hostaria Romanesca** (tel: 06-68864021) has good food for £15, outdoor tables and a superlative setting. Leave the Campo on Via dei Giubbonari and move on to Largo dei Librari 88, where you will come to **Filetti di Baccala** (tel: 06-6864018), which serves only deep-fried cod fillets and wine. At the end of that street cross Via Arenula to the Jewish area where **Sora Margherita** (Piazza delle Cinque Scole, 30, tel: 06-864002; lunchtime only Mon to Fri) offers good Jewish-Roman cuisine. This is a simple, inexpensive place around $15 (£10) for a full meal.

Across the river in Trastevere there are dozens of restaurants. If time is no object, you might want to wander randomly – but if there is a particular restaurant that you would like to visit, it could prove difficult to find in this maze of small streets (for restaurant tour of Trastevere, *see page 32*). For good, earthy food, **Augusto** (Piazza de Renzi 15), in a lovely square that is unfortunately heavily infested with cars, is highly

Left: a mouth-watering Roman menu

recommended. Augusto attracts an interesting mixture of locals and foreigners.

If you're planning a picnic, you can buy the necessary groceries in supermarkets at Tiburtina station (open 24 hours); Viale di Trastevere 60; Via Cola di Rienzo 173; and on Via Livorno at Piazza Bologna.

Restaurants

Other than traditional Roman cuisine, you can sample different regional dishes from all over the country. Classical Tuscan dishes are probably the most popular alternative.

Price Bands

$ – less than L25,000
$$ – L25-60,000
$$$ – more than L60,000
Prices are for a single meal without wine.

Ristorante Sant'Anna
Via di Sant' Anna 8
Tel: 06-68507190
Fresh fruit and vegetables from the stalls of nearby Campo de' Fiori supplemented with fish and seafood (bass, turbot, calamari) and extensive appetiser buffet. $$

Mario
Via della Vite 55
Tel: 06-6783818
The Tuscan fare is quite expensive, but the restaurant is well-placed in the Piazza di Spagna neighbourhood. $$

Dal Bolognese
Piazza del Popolo
Tel: 06-3611426
Both the cuisine and the style are high class. This is a touristy spot where diners go to see and be seen. $$$

Fortunato al Pantheon
Via del Pantheon 55
Tel: 06-6792788
Outdoor tables in famous setting. Popular with politicians. $$$

Sangallo
Vicolo della Vaccarella 11
Tel: 06-6865549
Not far from the Pantheon. The menu changes with the seasons, but all dishes are first-rate. Try the Texas beef with Gaeta olives. $$$

Note: The majority of restaurants that you will find in the Pantheon/Piazza Navona neighbourhood are expensive, but there are many cheaper spots on the nearby Via del Governo Vecchio.

La Tana dei Noantri
Via della Paglia 1
Tel: 06-5806404
La Tana dei Noantri is known for its somewhat expensive, traditional-style cuisine in a charming setting just off Piazza S Maria in Trastevere. $$$

Above: markets are the best source of fresh produce

Mary Meeting
Via Genova 20
Tel: 06-4881596
Fifty different pizzas, delicious desserts and
a specially bottled house wine. **$**

Taverna dei Quaranta
Via Claudia 24
Tel: 06-7000550
Near the Colosseum. Old-time Roman style.
Sample the fried codfish with apples and
zucchini. Vast wine list. **$$**

Sloppy Sam's
Campo De' Fiori 9
Tel: 06-8802637
Tasty sandwiches, soup and salads for lunch,
a live DJ every night. **$**

Papa Re
Via della Lungoretta 149
Tel: 06-5812069
Colourful, atmospheric, family-run estab-
lishment in Trastevere that serves traditional
Roman cuisine and features a guest guitarist
every night. **$$**

Al 16 da Raffaele e Stefano
Via del Portico d'Ottavia 16
Tel: 06-42880660
Opposite the synagogue. Outdoor tables in
garden. Specialities include roast lamb, ox-
tail and substantial salads. **$$**

Girarrosto Fiorentino
Via Sicilia 46
Tel: 06-42880660
Tuscan-style gourmet cuisine with prices
typical for the Via Veneto area. Extensive
wine list. **$$$**

La Campana
Vicolo della Campana 18
Tel: 06-6867820
Goethe once famously flirted with a waitress
in this 16th-century restaurant, the oldest in
Rome. Maybe he had sampled the artichoke
ravioli, as should you. **$$$**

Cesaretto
Via della Croce
No phone
A century-old former wine shop that es-
chews modernity, offers shared tables and
venerable Roman cuisine. **$$**

Quirino
Via delle Muratti 84
Tel: 06-69922509
Near Trevi Fountain since 1858. Sicilian cui-
sine with eggplant and succulent swordfish.
$$$

Pastarito
Via Cavour 59, tel: 06-4743773
Via Roma Libera 19, tel: 06-5883863
Endless pasta possibilities. **$**

Pizzarito
Also at Via Cavour 59, serves pizza. **$**

Smeraldo
Via Principe Amedeo 16
Tel: 06-483893
Light and airy eatery near Santa Maria Maggiore. Sample the veal scalloppini with porcini mushrooms. **$$**

Fiaschetteria Beltramme
Via delle Croce 39
No phone
Family cooking in historic tavern. **$**

Taverna Giulia
Vicolo dell' Oro 23
Tel: 06-6869768
Not far from Via Giulia. Serves Ligurian and regional specialities, such as stewed cod Genoa-style. **$$**

Le Maschere
Via Monte della Farina 29
Tel: 06-6879444
Extensive antipasto buffet followed by highly enticing Calabrian delicacies. **$–$$**

Crazy Bull Cafe
Via Mantora 56
Tel: 06-8845975
American 1950s décor in an old brewery building. Buffalo and shark steaks, Louisiana catfish, vegetarian fajitas. **$**

Alla Corte del Vino
Via Monte della Farina 43
Tel: 06-68307568
Wine bar with salamis, prosciutto and cheeses. **$**

Ethnic restaurants

The scope of Rome's restaurants has broadened. At least 200 Chinese, and scores of other ethnic restaurants have opened in the past few years, bringing the city up to date with other major capitals.

India House
Via Santa Cecilia 8
Tel: 06-5818508
Vegetarian and other set menus in this Trastevere restaurant. **$$**

Himalaya's Kashmir
Via Principe Amedeo 325
Tel: 06-4461972
Located just off Piazza Vittorio Emanuele, Himalaya's Kashmir features the exquisite specialities of India and Pakistan. **$$$**

ATM Sushi Bar
Villa della Penitenza 7
Tel: 06-68307053
Japanese chefs assiduously prepare the finest delicacies from the old country in almost austere surroundings near the Botanical Gardens in Trastevere. **$$–$$$**

Oliphant
Via delle Coppelle 31
Tel: 06-6881416
Traditionally popular Tex-Mex cuisine, including such perennials as fajitas, enchiladas, buffalo wraps and, of course, the ubiquitous barbecue. **$**

Sahara
Viale Ippocrate 43
Tel: 06-44242583
Spicy African (particularly Eritrean) food served communally with delicious honey wine on a spacious terrace. **$–$$**

Mesico e Nuvole
Via dei Magazzini Generali 8
Tel: 06-5741413
Tongue-tingling Mexican fare, lively atmosphere, outdoor terrace. **$–$$**

Birreria Viennese
Via della Croce 21
Tel: 06-6795569
Near Piazza di Spagna. Hungarian goulash, great bread and beer. **$**

Opening Times:

As a general rule, but with many exceptions, trattorias are closed on Sundays and restaurants on Mondays. Most establishments will serve lunch until about 3pm, and dinner from about 7pm. Trattorias tend to close at 10pm, and restaurants at 11pm or midnight. With occasional exceptions, you can eat outdoors from April to October.

Right: waiting for the rush

NIGHTLIFE

La dolce vita, the city's celebrated 'good life', is still lived in Rome, but no longer in the Via Veneto. Now *la dolce vita* centres on Trastevere, with elements in the area known as the Bermuda triangle, just off Piazza Navona, and in the Testaccio area around Monte dei Cocci (which has come a long way since the 3rd-century BC, when it was a rubbish dump).

Remember that Rome has two distinct seasons. It's winter from November to March (although there are days even in January when you can sit comfortably outside); and, with luck, summer begins in April. The hippest place for seeing and being seen by the young and trendy, **Gilda** (Via Mario de' Fiori 97, tel: 06-6784938), now has **Gilda on the Beach** at Fregene, a nearby seaside resort that's open only in the summer.

Nightlife in **Trastevere** focuses on an assortment of restaurants, wine bars and pubs, small clubs of all kinds – sometimes with live music, more often 'canned' – and tiny, intimate places in which to flirt and talk. The young hang out in the pizza parlours and pubs, the not-so-young in the wine bars. At 1am it all closes down.

To sample the nightlife in **Piazza Navona**,

take the small street leading from the sedate but touristy Tre Scalini bar and follow the scene as it unfolds, spilling in and out of various venues. It's a good idea to go with a local who knows the scene which, in Piazza Navona, continues until the early hours.

The **Testaccio** scene (ask your taxi driver to take you to 'Il Mattatoio', the slaughterhouse, and start roving) begins around 11pm, lasts all night and attracts a wilder kind of reveller, including the transvestite crowd. Most 'trans', as they are known, come from Brazil. These beautiful creatures of the night sell (for £15–35/$22–50) the most unashamed sex in town. They usually have impossibly long legs, silicon breasts and, to the great surprise of the naive and uninitiated, a male member hidden under those miniskirts. While many enjoy this entertaining scene, it is not for the prudish.

If you come to Rome between mid-June and mid-September you'll be able to enjoy the annual festival called **Estate Romana**. This features open-air movies (screened at Tiber Island, Celio Hill and other venues around town); plays staged at the Gianicolo hill's outdoor theatres – which have a fine view of the city as a backdrop – and at the Quercia del Tasso (Greek and Roman works); operas at the Caracalla Baths; classical-music concerts held in courtyards, churches and palaces (including the splendid setting of the ancient Theatre of Marcello); and soul, blues and rap gigs centred on the Testaccio area. In Trastevere there are now almost 50 pubs, many of them open until 2am, the oldest and most famous being **La Scala** in Via della Scala.

Practical Tips

English-language listings can be found in *Wanted in Rome*. On Thursdays, the newspaper *La Repubblica* issues a supplement called 'Roma', which publishes comprehensive entertainment listings, with addresses, phone numbers and schedules. Not that spontaneity-loving Romans book for anything except the opera and some theatre. Be prepared to pay at least L50,000, drinks included, in the course of an evening out. Concerts (classical and rock), dance and discos might set you back even more. Live jazz in Rome has a very good reputation.

Left: the Spanish Steps at night

Classical Music and Dance

You will come across choral performances in churches throughout the city. The major venues for serious music include the **Santa Cecilia auditorium** (tel: 68801044), the **Foro Italico** and the **Teatro dell'Opera** (tel: 06-48160255). The Rome Philharmonic Academy presents concerts in the Teatro Olimpico (tel: 06-32011752); the Sacred Music Society at Chiesa di S Ignazio (tel: 06-68805816) and the Goethe Institute at Teatro Colosseo (tel: 06-7004932).

Summer is the time for outdoor concerts, including a festival at the **Caracalla Baths**. In July, there are concerts in the grounds of **Villa Giulia** and the cloisters of **Santa Maria della Pace**. The season's orchestral concerts take place around the **Teatro di Marcello** (tel: 06-77209128), at the **Villa Pamphili** (tel: 06-77072842) and also in the **Pincio Gardens**. The quality of the music – and the concerts' glorious settings – are such that a lot of people travel long distances, even from abroad, to attend.

Rock, Jazz and Folk Music

Big rock concerts are held at the **Palazzetto dello Sport**, a covered arena holding 20,000, and at soccer stadiums with capacities of around 60,000. On a smaller scale, two venues in the Testaccio area, **Il Mattatoio** and **Villaggio Globale**, regularly host gigs by local Italian bands and groups from Africa, Asia and elsewhere. Turn up early.

Uonna (Via Cassia 871), the in-place in the 1970s, is still going strong on a steady diet of hard rock, grunge, trash, punk, reggae and rap. To get in you have to be a member (you can buy instant membership at the door) and it's an expensive taxi ride (about €10/$15) from the city centre.

There's blues and rock every night from 9pm at the cosy **Big Mama** (Vicolo San Francesco a Ripa, in Trastevere, tel: 06-5812551), and also at **The Blues Temple**, tel: 06-5812551).

Off the beaten track but worth seeking out is **Forte Prenestino**, a splendid fort occupied by politically minded squatters, where occasional rock concerts are held in a unique setting. **Alpheus** (Via del Commercio 36, tel: 06-5747826), is one of the biggest and best-organised venues. Here you can dance to quite different kinds of music in the same building: three levels occupy over 2,000 sq metres (nearly 22,000 sq ft) of space, and meals are available if you get hungry. Alpheus is good for jazz, as are **Il Castello** and lots of smaller places, such as **Mississippi Blues**, **Saint Louis Music City** (Via del Cardello 13), **Ciao Musica** and **Caffè Les Folies**. None of these clubs and pubs have regular schedules.

Rome's temple of folk music is **Folkstudio**, which opened in the early 1960s in

Trastevere with Giancarlo Cesaroni. Also good for folk sounds are the recently-opened **Shamrock** in the Colosseum neighbourhood, and **Fonklea** (where you can also eat) near St Peter's. Irish and American folk are particularly popular in Rome. In Campo di Fiori, the **Drunken Ship** (tel: 06-68300535) is a Brit-style bar that attracts a mixed crowd. The entertainment here sometimes includes unscheduled jam sessions.

Movies, Theatre, Opera, Dance

Only one cinema, the twin-auditorium **Pasquino** (Vicolo del Piede, Trastevere), screens English-language movies four times daily, almost every day. Not far away, **the Alcatraz** (tel: 06-5880099) is a small, arty cinema that features English-language movies on Mondays.

Of the cineclubs that show vintage movie classics, the best is **Azzurro Scipioni** (Via Scipioni 84, tel: 06-39737161) in the Vatican area. It screens six movies a day in its twin theatres (at 6.30, 8.30 and 10.30pm)

Above: black rules at night

Other Nightlife

Piper 90 (Via Tagliamento 9, tel: 06-841 4459) is the oldest, most famous rock/disco venue. It also has a video theatre.

English-speaking Romans gravitate towards the **Blu Bar** (Via dei Soldati 25) and the **Little Bar** (Via Gregoriana 54a), but the trendiest place is **the Hemingway** (an American bar in Roman style) followed closely by **the Zelig**. Also in the running are **Caffè della Pace**, on the street of that name, and **Le Cornacchie** (Piazza Ronadini 53), both near Piazza Navona.

There are two lively Celtic pubs: **Mad Jack's** (Via Arenula 20, tel: 06-68806223) and **the Nag's Head**, near Piazza Venezia. **Open Gate** and **Notorius** (tel 06-42010572) are trendy, but neither is cheap; expect to go through £75/$110 in a night, or £30/$45 if you're really careful.

The hottest clubs for young people are the **Alien** (Via Velletri 13, tel: 06-68806223) and **Stardust** (Vicolo de Renzi, Trastevere), which comes alive after midnight.

Circolo degli Artisti (Via Lamarmora 28, near the station) stages avant-garde concerts, while **Blue Zone** (Via Campania 37a) and **Le Stelle** (Via C. Beccaria 22) warm up at around 3am and keep going until dawn. **The Maghreb** (Piazza Cestia, by the Pyramid) is a lively African restaurant which also has music. But the real 'in' place is **Il Locale** (Vicolodel Fico, tel: 06-6879075), which hosts a different band every evening. Next door, and also worth visiting, is a crazily decorated piano bar, **Jonathan's Angels** (via della Fossa 18, tel: 06-6893426). The **Piper** (Via Taplisimento 9, tel: 06-8414459), tends to follow rather than establish trends, but has been popular for more than 30 years.

The gay night scene in Rome is very active, with **Alibi** (Via di Monte Testaccio 44, tel: 06-5743448) being the most famous spot. **Angelo Azzurro** (Via Card. Merry del Val 13) is also the centre of a lively scene. You could begin your evening at the Hangar bar (Via in Selci 69) and keep your ears open for what's happening on that particular night.

Women looking for Mr Right might find him at **Panico** (Via di Panico 13) on Sundays and at **Galaxia** (Piazza Bulgarelli 41) on Fridays and Sundays.

and, for an entrance fee of £7/$10, you gain admission to all areas. The small and cosy theatres are beautifully organised by Silvano Agosti, himself a film director, and his family. Another good cineclub is **Nuovo Sacher** (tel: 06-5818116) in Trastevere. Run by the director Nanni Moretti, it features a bar and bookshop and also sells movies. Not surprisingly, this is a popular haunt among movie buffs and the intelligentsia, and in summer it moves outdoors.

As for theatre, there are frequent visits by English companies that stage outdoor performances at the tiny Quercia del Tasso, at the top of the Gianicolo Hill, and at Ostia Antica (*see page 67*), where performances take place in the old Roman amphitheatre. Both can be inspiring experiences.

Italians are known for their love of children, and theatres that stage performances of interest to youngsters include the **Accettella Teatro Mongiovino** (Via G Benocchi 25, tel: 06-5739405), and **Teatro Le Maschere** (Via A Saliceti 1, tel: 06-58330817).

There are regular dramatic and musical events in the **Teatro Olimico** (Piazza G Da Fabrioso 17, tel: 06-32011752); at **Teatro Valle** (tel: 06-68803794); and at **Teatro Di Roma** (Lungotevere dei Papareschi, tel: 06-6880461), among many others.

Opera in Rome has two seasons: from November to January at the **Teatro dell'Opera** and, in summer, at the **Caracalla Baths**. If you fancy a night at the opera, don't forget to make prior reservations.

Above: transvestite clubs feature performers from Brazil
Right: street celebrations are a part of Roman life

CALENDAR OF EVENTS

January

Christmas fair in Piazza Navona, ending with the witch festival *Epiphany (befana)* on 6 January, during which good children are given gifts while the naughty receive sweets shaped like coal.
La Festa di Sant'Antonio Abate features blessings for animals in the church of Sant'Eusebio all'Esquillino.

February–March

Towns in Castelli Romani hold street processions to mark *Carnevale*.
La Festa di San Giuseppi (St Joseph's Day) is celebrated on 19 March, especially around the church of the same name.

April

Easter is the time for pilgrimages and concerts. On Good Friday, the pope leads a mass at the Colosseum, and a procession passes the stations of the cross. The pope gives his *Urbi et Orbi* address on Easter morning.
The arrival of spring is celebrated by *La Festa della Primavera*.

May

May Day features a huge free concert in front of San Giovanni in Laterano.
The *Italian Open Tennis Championships* are held in the first week; the *International Horse Show* at the end of the month.
The two twice-yearly arts and crafts fairs of *La Fiera d'Arte di Via Margutta* and *La Mostra dell'Antiquariato* are held in late May and late October.

June

The founders of the Catholic church are honoured on 29 June by the *San Pietro e San Paolo* holiday. Special masses are held in their basilicas.
The famous summer-long *Estate Romana* features a varied programme of concerts, plays, movies and performances.

July

The Trastevere street festival of *Festa dei Noantri* runs to mid-August.
Outdoor *opera* at the Baths of Caracalla.
The *Roma Alta Moda* fashion shows exhibit the season's top new lines

August

Simulated snow falls on *La Festa della Madonna della Neve*, which commemorates the founding of the Basilica of Santa Maria Maggiore, on 5 August.

December

Settimana dei Beni Culturali at the start of the month is marked by free entry to all state-run museums and historical sites.
The Immaculate Conception (*Immacolata Concezione*) is celebrated on 8 December in Piazza di Spagna.
At *Christmas* the streets are decorated and many churches put on nativity scenes.

Practical Information

GETTING THERE

By Air

There are frequent direct scheduled flights to Rome from most major European cities, from Australia and from a number of cities in North America. There are also charter flights from much of Europe.

Travellers on scheduled flights land at the main airport, Aeroporto Leonardo da Vinci in Fiumicino, about 30km (18 miles) southwest of Rome (**Fiumicino airport**, tel: 06-595 or 06-4455). Some flights arrive at Ciampino airport, about 15km (9 miles) to the southeast (**Ciampino airport**, tel: 06-94947). From here a bus travels to the Anagnina Metro station.

By Rail

There are train services to Rome from all over Italy and from northern Europe.

If you are travelling from the UK, note that the cost of a train ticket is approximately the same as the airfare, so it's only worth travelling by train if you have time to spare of if you intend to stop off along the way.

Most trains arrive at the main Roman station, Termini. Motorail trains use Stazione Tiburtina to the northeast of the centre, as do some trains on the north–south line (incorporating Bologna, Florence and Naples).

By Bus

If you are travelling by bus, you will almost certainly arrive at or near the Stazione Termini. Most European coach companies, as well as the Italian ones (Lazzi Express, Appian Line and COTRAL), use the Piazza dei Cinquecento as their terminus.

By Road

Car travellers arriving in Rome from any direction first hit the Gran Raccordo Anulare (GRA), the ring motorway. The A1 (Autostrada del Sole) leads into the GRA from both north and south, as does the A24 from the east. If you arrive on the Via del Mare from the coast (Ostia), you can either join the GRA or continue straight into the city centre.

The various roads into the centre lead off the GRA. Study the map and choose your exit according to the part of the city you are heading for. For the north, choose the exits Via Salaria, Via Flaminia or Via Nomentana. If heading for the Vatican area, follow the GRA to the west and take the exit Via Aurelia. If you're going south, take the Via Tuscolana, Via Appia Nuova, Via Pontina (which leads into the Via Cristoforo Colombo) or the Via del Mare.

When leaving the GRA, follow the white signs to the road you want rather than the blue ones, which usually lead away from the centre. Look out for the city-centre sign: a black dot in the middle of a black circle on a white background.

TRAVEL ESSENTIALS

Climate

Average daytime temperatures in Rome:

Jan: 7.5°C (46°F)	Feb: 8.8°C (48°F)
Mar: 10.8°C (51°F)	Apr: 14.2°C (58°F)
May: 18.2°C (65°F)	June: 22.3°C (72°F)
July: 24.9°C (77°F)	Aug: 24.6°C (76°F)
Sept: 21.3°C (70°F)	Oct: 16.8°C (62°F)
Nov: 12.8°C (55°F)	Dec: 8.7°C (48°F)

Left: light and shadows on the street
Right: a popular form of transport

WHEN TO VISIT

The best time to visit Rome is in the spring or autumn. In winter you'll have the major sites all to yourself, but the weather can be forbidding. July is pleasantly warm, but the city is already crowded. In August it's hot and humid and many shops are closed. The Estate Romana festival takes place from mid-July to mid-September, with movies screened and music performed in open-air settings, close to or in historical sites.

Clothing

Rome is a fairly formal city so be warned that shorts and T-shirts are looked at askance, except on the beach. In the Vatican and in all churches, men and women are expected to wear long trousers and long sleeves.

MONEY MATTERS

You will need Italian lire to leave both the airport and the station, so either buy some before you leave home, or get change as soon as you arrive. Banks open weekdays 8.30am–1.30pm and 2.45–3.45pm. The two banks at Termini remain open until 5pm. When changing money, go to mainstream banks or exchange offices displaying No Commission signs. (Commission can be 4 percent or more.)

American Express travellers cheques and cash can be exchanged at major post offices.

GETTING AROUND

Airport Connections

From Fiumicino airport, trains run to the central stations Ostiense and Termini every 30 minutes until 10pm. There is also an infrequent late-night bus service. If you take a taxi, choose only a yellow or white one with a meter. Be prepared to pay a taxi fare of £35–40 ($50–60) to your hotel from Fiumicino; £6–15 ($9–22) from Termini or Ostiense. From Ciampino airport, a COTRAL bus runs hourly to the Anagrina Metro station. You can order a radio taxi by phone (Tel: 06-3570 or 06-4994).

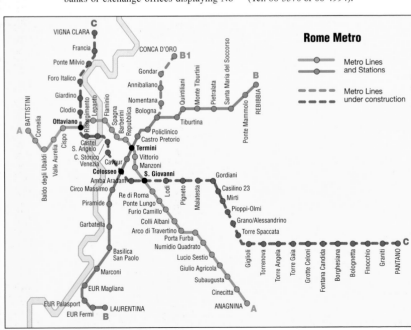

Rome Metro

Metro Lines and Stations

Metro Lines under construction

Taxis, Buses, Trams and Metro

Meters in yellow and white taxis tend to start at around L5,000, with a short trip costing £3.50 ($5 or so), a medium one, £6 ($9). After 10pm and on Sundays there is an additional surcharge. Pay only what's on the meter plus 5 percent tip.

Tobacco stores displaying a big **T** sell bus tickets, without which you are not supposed to board a bus. There's a fine if you're caught without a ticket or without having stamped it in a machine near the rear door.

Bus lines (and some trains) are operated by COTRAL (tel: 167-431784, free). Bus stops advertise routes with yellow metal displays that feature a red circle around the place you're at. You can obtain a comprehensive list of bus and tram lines from the ATAC booth in Piazza dei Cinquecentro, opposite Termini station. A three-hour sightseeing bus tour leaves Termini at 3.30pm every day in summer, and at weekends in winter. From Termini, the 64 bus travels to Piazza Venezia and then to the Vatican, by way of Piazza Novona and the Pantheon.

The Metro is a skeletal system with only two lines, A and B, intersecting at Termini. Unless you are going to the seaside it is not very useful for tourists, although Line B connects Termini and Piramides stations. From Piramides you can catch the train to Ostia (though sometimes you need to change at Magliana) or get the 280 bus to Trastevere. For more information, contact **Transport Information** (tel: 800-431784, weekdays).

Trains

Should you want to leave the city by train, you will find Termini station a frustrating experience with long queues at the enquiries and ticket desks. You are likely to get better, more reliable service from the city's travel agencies. After buying a ticket, you must stamp it at one of the yellow machines found all around the stations.

The left-luggage office, near the ticket windows, is open from 5am to midnight.

Driving

Driving a car through Rome's tangled streets can be an exercise in frustration. On the positive side, the state tourist office offers discount coupons that subsidise the cost of

petrol. Ask your home country's automobile club how to get a *Pachetto Italia* packet of these coupons.

Rental cars are available from:
Hertz (tel: 322-5240)
Maggiore (1478-67067)
Avis (650-11531)
Europcar (650-10879)

If you have the confidence to rent a scooter, call, Hertz: 322-5240. For a limousine service for airport pick-up and tours of Rome, contact International (tel: 041-2770580; fax: 5208396).

HOURS & HOLIDAYS

Official Holidays
1 January New Year's Day
6 January Epiphany
Easter
25 April Liberation Day
1 May May Day
Whit Sunday (Monday not a holiday)
15 August The Assumption of Mary
1 November All Souls' Day
8 December Feast of the Immaculate Conception
25–26 December Christmas

Holidays and Festivals
New Year's Eve is very big business in Rome: drinking, dancing, noisy midnight celebrations with firecrackers. It falls in the middle of a long holiday period that starts the day before Christmas and lasts until Epiphany on 6 January. Those staying in Rome often visit the annual Christmas Market in Piazza Navona.

Easter is normally a three- or four-day holiday. Italians say that Christmas you spend with your family; Easter with whomever you want. On Good Friday there's a procession from the Palatine to the Colosseum. On Easter Sunday, many people head for St Peter's Square at noon for the pope's traditional *Urbi et Orbi* blessing. The saints' days of St Joseph (19 March) and St John (23 June) are celebrated with special dishes.

The city empties in August. Roman families head for the sea, north or south according to budget, class or the location of their second home. One family in three has a home at the seaside or in the village from which they came. Rome's population has exploded over the past 50 years, with new arrivals mostly from southern Italy. When people leave for their second homes on weekends, the city is noticeably less hectic. It's a good idea to take advantage of this.

Opening Times

Most of the smaller shops and bars, as well as churches (but excluding restaurants), follow the traditional 'split' day. That is, they are open from 8 or 9am until about 1pm, then close for a few hours before reopening at about 3.30 or 4pm. Virtually all small outlets are closed on Sundays and many don't open until late in the afternoon on Mondays.

There are three types of museum in Rome: those operated by the state, by the town hall and of course those found in the Vatican. Museums in the first two categories are open 9am–7pm (closed Mon); those in the Vatican, 8.45am–3.45pm (closed Sun).

In the more up-market, touristy areas, shops open at about 9 or 9.30am and continue to serve customers, with no siesta break, until late in the evening. The American concept of 24-hour consumerism is, however, alien to Italians – you will rarely find a shop that's open even late at night.

ACCOMMODATION

It's a good idea to stay in a hotel near the city centre. This way you will save time, taxi fares and, not least, a lot of energy – in Rome you will almost certainly want to do a lot of walking. The best areas for hotels are around the up-market Piazza del Popolo and Piazza Navona. The district around the Termini station suffers a surfeit of traffic, but is considerably cheaper. Here you'll find a multiethnic mixture of *extra comunitari* (the Italian expression for people from non-European countries), who together form something of a town within a town.

When in Rome, so the saying goes, do as the Romans do. If you really want to live like a Roman, and experience the full impact of all that history, you should stay in a neighbourhood near the great ancient monuments. Whether you are a budget traveller content with a spartan room, or a high-class holidaymaker or business traveller desirous of more elegant surroundings, you'll *know* you're in Rome when, on walking out of your hotel, you find yourself in front of the Pantheon or Piazza di Spagna or Navona, or in one of the narrow, medieval streets that lead to a classical square.

In the following list, the price codes are as follows:

$ – up to $75 (£50)
$$ – $75–150 (£50–100)
$$$ – $150–270 (£100–180)
$$$$ – over $270 (over £180)

Prices refer to the cheapest double room with private facilities (where available).

Left: small hotels can be the friendliest

Near Fiumicino

Cervia
Via Cervi 39
Tel: 06-66560657
Restaurant, bar. $

Venosta
Via Carbonia 230
Tel: 06-6671264
Restaurant, bar, beach. $$

Motel Corsi
Via Aurelia km 27
Tel: 06-61697021; fax: 06-61697443
Restaurant, bar, transport to airport. $$$

Near Termini Station

Perugia
Via del Colosso 7
Tel: 06-6797200; Fax: 06-6784635
Simple, no frills. $

Piave
Via Piave 14
Tel: 06-4743447; Fax: 06-4873360
Lobby bar. Some bathless rooms. $

Trento
Via Panisperna 95
Tel: 06-4745213; Fax: 06-4845218
Ten rooms, some without bath. $

Piazza di Spagna area

Campo de Fiori
Via del Biscione 6
Tel: 06-68806865; Fax: 06-6676003
Old house with terrace over busy square. $$

Pomezia
Via del Chiavari 12
Tel: 06-8861371
Near Campo de'Fiori. Breakfast included. $$

Aventino
Via S Domenico 10
Tel: 06-5743547; Fax: 06-5783604
Tranquil garden. Breakfast included. $–$$

Sheraton Golf
Viale Parco de' Medici 165
Tel: 06-658588; Fax: 06-6858742
Enjoys sedate surroundings of lakes and lawns. Tennis, pool, golf. $$$$

Central

Abruzzi
Piazza del Rotonda 69
Tel: 06-6792021
Overlooks the Pantheon. $

Borromeo
Via Cavour 117
Tel: 06-485856; Fax: 06-4882541
Stylish, elegant rooms; marble bathrooms.
Bar. $$–$$$

Castellino al Pialo Blanco
Via Cesare Battisti 133
Tel: 06-6679977; Fax: 06-6790036
Century-old hotel near Piazza Venezia, complete with frescoes, paintings and flowers. $$

Forum
Via Tor de' Conti 25
Tel: 06-6792446; Fax: 06-6786479
In quiet street overlooking Trajan's Market.
Restaurant, bar. $$$

Marcus
Via del Clemeninto 94
Tel: 06-6873679; Fax: 06-830320
Elegantly furnished small hotel in centuries-old building near Piazza Navona. $$

Navona
Via dei Sedari 8
Tel: 06-6864203; Fax: 06-68803802
Some rooms have bath. $

Parlamento
Via delle Conventite 5
Tel (and Fax): 06-69921000
Friendly management; 29 a/c rooms with
TV and breakfast included. $

Raphael
Largo Febo 2
Tel: 06-682831; fax: 06-6878993
Luxury without pomp. Rooms with ancient
and modern sculpture. $$$

Sole al Pantheon
Via del Pantheon 63
Tel: 06-6780441; fax: 06-69940689
The rooms, with painted ceilings, have
hosted poets, artists and celebrities for five
centuries. Jacuzzis. $$$

Trevi
Vicolo del Barbuccio 20
Tel: 06-6789563; Fax: 06-6994107
Remodeled mansion near famous fountain.
Breakfast included. $$

Venezia
Via Varese 18
Tel: 06-4457101; Fax: 06-4957687
Meticulously run hotel with antique furnishings, classical music and wild flowers. $$

Via de Veneto area

Lord Byron
Via G de Notaria 5
Tel: 06-3220404; Fax: 06-3220405
Stylish member of the Leading Hotels
Group. Restaurant and piano bar. $$$$

Piazza di Spagna area

Gregoriana
Via Gregoriana 18
Tel: 06-6794269; Fax: 06-6784258
Art Deco interior. Near Spanish Steps. $$

Hassler
Piazza Trinita dei Monti 6.
Tel: 06-699340; Fax: 06-6789991
Top of its class and atop the Spanish Steps.
Bedrooms with Venetian glass chandeliers
and marble bathrooms. Elegant rooftop
restaurant. $$$$

Inghilterra
Via Bocca di Leone 14
Tel: 06-69981; Fax: 06-69922243
Since opening in 1850, its clients have included Hemingway and many other writers, artists and musicians who have adored
its clubby English ambience. $$$$

Scalinata Di Spagna
Piazza Trinita dei Monti 17
Tel: 06-6793006; Fax: 06-9940598
A 19th-century hotel at the top of the Spanish Steps. $$$

Margutta
Via Laurina 34
Tel: 06-3223674; Fax: 06-3200395
In a quiet street just off Piazza del Popolo,
its best rooms are those at the top that share
a roof terrace. Book well in advance. $$

Hotel Des Artistes
Via Villafranca 20
Tel: 06-4454365; Fax: 06-4462368
27 rooms, near to Termini station. $–$$$

Campo dei Fiori area

Some of the small hotels in this neighbourhood have accommodated pilgrims since the
Middle Ages. Around the traditional old
bustling marketplace, the streets are named
after ancient trades (*Giubbonari* means
jacket makers; *Chiavari*, nail makers; *Cappellari*, hat makers) that are still practised
in countless ground floor *bottegas*.

Della Lunetta
Piazza del Paradiso 68
Tel: 06-6861080; Fax: 06-4462368
Situated in an old but interesting square, this
establishment has 36 rooms, either with or
without a bath. $

Piccolo
Via dei Chiavari 32
Tel: 06-68802580
An old favourite with seasoned travellers.
Small, fairly cheap and reliable. $

Rinascimento
Via del Pellegrino 122
Tel: 06-6874813; Fax: 06-6833518
Centrally located in a street with three book
stores, one specialising in travel. $$

Smeraldo
Vivolo dei Chiarodoli 11
Tel: 06-6875929; Fax: 06-68805495
Don't be fooled by the garish entrance: this
is a simple, 35-room establishment which
fills up fast, so book early. $$

Right: the stone portal of an old hotel

Sole
Via del Biscione 76
Tel: 06-68806873; Fax: 06-6893787
Characterful old place with garden. A quiet haven, it is often booked up, so call well ahead of your visit to be sure of a room. **$$**

Trastevere area

Carmel
Via Mameli 11
Tel: 06-5809921
Ten spotless rooms. No children. **$**

Hotel Trastevere
Via Manara 25
Tel: 06-5814713
Close to the heart of Trastevere but relatively unknown. Overlooks market. **$**

Vatican area

Alimandi
Via Tunisi 8
Tel: 06-39723948; Fax: 06-39723943
A *pensione* situated very close to St Peter's. 35 rooms plus a spacious roof terrace. **$**

Columbus
Via della Conciliazione 33
Tel: 06-6865435; Fax: 06-6864874
Once a monastery on the wide, showy street leading to St Peter's. Still has frescoes and a walled garden. **$$$**

Via Veneto area

For the most part, this famous area lacks its former glamour, but it retains its old hotels, two of which are grand indeed.

Excelsior
Via Vittorio Veneto 125
Tel: 06-4708; Fax: 06-4826205
Nearly 400 luxurious rooms, much imitation marble, silk-lined corridors and abundant chandeliers all contribute to a dramatic if slightly passé theatrical setting. **$$$$**

Majestic
Via Veneto 50
Tel: 06-486841; Fax: 06-4880984
Almost a century old, with an impressive guest list that has included, in recent years, Pavarotti and Madonna. An extravagant indulgence if you can afford it. **$$$$**

HEALTH & EMERGENCIES

There is no charge at hospitals' first-aid departments, so in case of unexpected trouble or an accident, don't hesitate to head for the nearest hospital. It might be quicker to take a taxi there than to wait for an ambulance to arrive. The city's famous oldest hospital (tel: 06-5873299), situated on the island in the River Tiber, has been operating, in more senses than one, for 2,200 years.

There's an excellent private clinic in a beautiful setting on top of the Gianicolo hill called the **Salvator Mundi** (Viale Mura Gianicolenei 67–77, tel: 06-586041). The staff here speak English and are fast, efficient and reliable. Go there if you can possibly afford it.

For late-night pharmacies try: Piazza del Cinquecento (tel: 06-4880019) near Termini; Corso Vittorio Emanuele 343 (tel: 06-688-01408); and Via Nazionale 228 (tel: 06-4880754). All are on the 18N bus route.

Pharmacies display the familiar red or green cross and can be found all over town. Quite a few offer homeopathic remedies. Call 1921 for details such as opening hours, or check a pharmacy window for details of the nearest pharmacy that's open.

For 24-hour medical assistance, tel: 06-47498 or (at night) 06-4826741. If you need emergency dental care, the Dental Centre Viminale (Via Palermo 28, tel: 06-484863) has English-speaking staff.

The various embassies can refer you to doctors who speak your language. If you lose your passport, money or valuables, you should inform your embassy. Police buses with multilingual staff are situated at many points around the city.

Be wary of deft pickpockets and leave valuables at home or in the hotel safe. Be wary of women with young children who approach with a piece of cardboard or a newspaper extended in your direction. They may try to crowd you, confuse you, and then run off with your valuables. Be aware also that women's bags can be easily snatched by boys passing on motorcycles.

Lost or stolen credit cards:
AmEx (06-72280371)
Visa (800-877232)
MasterCard (800-870866)
Diner's Club (800-864064)

Useful Telephone Numbers

Police: 113
Police (Foreigners' Bureau): 06-468629
Traffic police: 5544
Medical emergencies: 118
Ambulances: 5100 (for Red Cross)
Postal enquiries: 180
Directory listings: 12
Operator: 170
Long distance: 184

COMMUNICATIONS & MEDIA

Telephone

Only a few public telephones still accept coins (one 200-lire piece or two 100-lire coins) and occasionally you'll find phones that accept both coins and cards. But mostly you'll find phones that accept only cards, so be prepared with one in advance. Tobacconists (identified with a big, black **T**) sell phone cards (L5,000 or L10,000) as well as stamps and other such useful items.

To dial abroad, first dial the outgoing code 00, then the country code: Australia (61), France (33), Germany (49), Japan (81), Netherlands (31), Spain (34), UK (44), US and Canada (1) and so forth. If you are using a US credit phone card, dial the company's access number: Sprint, 172-1877; AT&T 172-1011; MCI, 172-1022.

Since 1998 it has been necessary to dial the 06 prefix for Rome even when you are calling from within the city.

Postal Service

The main post office on Piazza San Silvestro is open until 9pm on weekdays and until noon at weekends. There are more than 100 branch offices, open until 2pm. Stamps can be bought at tobacconists bearing the **T** sign.

A recent innovation is the implementation of a priority mail service which guarantees 24-hour delivery anywhere in Italy.

Foreign Newspapers

All the major tourist spots have newsstands that carry foreign-language newspapers and magazines. Papers published in London are more easily found in Rome than are their American counterparts (with the exceptions of *USA Today* and the *Wall Street Journal*). The Paris edition of the same day's *Herald Tribune* is usually available by midday. The two best kiosks in town are in the Via Veneto and remain open until 2am.

What's On

Two English-language fortnightlies, *Wanted in Rome* (which carries information for all Italy) and *Roma'cè* (in Italian with an English section) are available at newsstands. Also check out *Roma*, a Thursday supplement with the daily *La Repubblica*.

USEFUL INFORMATION

Photography

Some museums and tourist sites impose a charge for taking photographs, but only if they see your camera. Various others, including the Vatican museums, ban photography altogether. Nobody is allowed to take pictures in the Sistine Chapel.

The Pope

From November to February, the pope's general audiences usually take place at 11am on Wednesdays in the audience chamber. During the rest of the year they tend to occur in the afternoon in St Peter's Square.

Above: papal mail
Right: Roma is 'amor' spelt backwards

Requests for tickets can be made from the Prefetto della Casa Pontificia, whose office is through the bronze door (Portone di Bronzo) at the right of the basilica. Tickets are usually issued on Tuesday and Wednesday mornings. On Sundays the pope gives a blessing from his study window over to the right-hand side of St Peter's Square. If you want to visit the Vatican Gardens, apply at the office on the left of the square (tel: 06-6984466) where most questions concerning Vatican City can be answered.

During the summer, the pope is frequently at Castel Gandolfo in the Castelli hills south of Rome (for information, call 06-9360340). In most bookstores you will find a fold-up poster called *I Sommi Pontefici Romani* ('The Roman Pontiffs') that lists in English all 264 popes from St Peter to John Paul II (elected in 1978). Costing about $6, it contains a few lines about each pope – birthplace, background, date of election – and contains quite a few surprises in its small print.

USEFUL ADDRESSES

Tourist Information
Ente Provinciale per il Turismo, Via Parigi 5, near Termini station, or, more helpful, the **CIT office** at Piazza della Repubblica 68, in Viale de Trastevere, near the post office, east Garibaldi Bridge. www.informaroma.it

Tourist Information Abroad
Italian State Tourist Office: 1 Princes Street, London W1R 8AY, England. Tel: 020-7408 1254; fax: 020-7493-6695.

Italian Government Tourist Office: 630 Fifth Ave, New York 10111, USA. Tel: (212) 245-4822; fax: 586-9249.

Consulates
Australia
Corso Trieste 25, tel: 06-852721.
UK
Via XX Settembre 80a, tel: 06-4825441
Canada
Via Zara 30, tel: 06-44598421.
Ireland
Piazza Campitelli 3, tel: 06-6979121
USA
Via Vittorio Veneto, tel: 06-46741
Japan
Via Q Sello 60, tel: 06-487991
Germany
Via S Martino della Battaglia 4, tel: 06-492-131
Spain
Via Campo Marzio 34, tel: 06-6871401

FURTHER READING

Insight Guide: Rome (Apa Publications, 1998). This thoroughly revised edition has numerous new, detailed maps and wonderful images.
D H Lawrence and Italy (Viking Penguin, 1972)
Rome: The Sweet Tempestuous Life by Paul Hofmann (Congdon & Weed, 1984)
The Ides of March by Thornton Wilder (Harper & Row, 1948)
The Agony and the Ecstasy by Irving Stone (Doubleday, 1961)

INSIGHT
Pocket Guides

Insight Pocket Guides pioneered a new approach to guidebooks, introducing the concept of the authors as "local hosts" who would provide readers with personal recommendations, just as they would give honest advice to a friend who came to stay. They also included a full-size pull-out map. Now, to cope with the needs of the 21st century, new editions in this growing series are being given a new look to make them more practical to use, and restaurant and hotel listings have been greatly expanded.

The travel guides that replace a tour guide – now better than ever with more listings and a fresh new design

☀ INSIGHT GUIDES

The world's largest collection of visual travel guides

Now in association with

Discovery CHANNEL

ACKNOWLEDGEMENTS

Photography	**Frances Gransden** *and*
10, 15, 16T	**AKG**
12B, 45T	**Ping Amranand**
20, 34T, 36B, 51, 63, 64, 81	**Patrizia Giancotti**
8/9, 52	**Jim Holmes**
30, 39, 40, 48T, 53, 54, 75, 76, 78, 90	**Elvira d'Ippoliti**
13	**Mary Evans Picture Library**
6B, 65, 66	**Gerd Pfeifer**
34B, 42, 47, 62	**Mark Auriel Rettenbacher**
Cover	**Tony Stone Images/Simone Hubert**
Back Cover	**Frances Gransden**
Production	**Tanvir Virdee**
Design	**Carlotta Junger**
Cartography	**Maria Donnelly** *and*
	Berndtson & Berndtson

INDEX